LOOKING DOWN ON WAR

EVOLUTION OF AIRBORNE OPS

Imagery from WWII Intelligence files

Colonel Roy M. Stanley II, USAF (ret.)

Pen & Sword
AVIATION

Other Books by the Author

Second World War Photo Intelligence
Prelude To Pearl Harbor
To Fool A Glass Eye
Asia From Above
V-Weapons Hunt
Axis Warships
The Normandy Invasion

First published in Great Britain in 2015 by
PEN & SWORD AVIATION
an imprint of
Pen & Sword Books Ltd,
47 Church Street,
Barnsley, South Yorkshire
S70 2AS

Copyright © Colonel Roy M. Stanley II 2015

ISBN 978 1 47384 380 6

Typeset by CHIC GRAPHICS

Printed and bound in Malta by Gutenberg Press Ltd.

Pen & Sword Books Ltd incorporates the Imprints of
Pen & Sword Aviation, Pen & Sword Family History, Pen & Sword Maritime, Pen & Sword Military, Pen & Sword Discovery, Wharncliffe Local History, Wharncliffe True Crime, Wharncliffe Transport, Pen & Sword Select, Pen & Sword Military Classics, Leo Cooper, The Praetorian Press, Remember When, Seaforth Publishing and Frontline Publishing.

For a complete list of Pen & Sword titles please contact
PEN & SWORD BOOKS LIMITED
47 Church Street, Barnsley, South Yorkshire, S70 2AS, England
E-mail: enquiries@pen-and-sword.co.uk
Website: www.pen-and-sword.co.uk

CONTENTS

ACKNOWLEDGEMENTS

This book could not have been finished without contributions from three remarkable and talented women—my wife and tireless caregiver/editor, Mary Ellen; Susan Strange, NARA researcher extraordinaire who could find the Lost Ark for me if I asked (www.Strange Archives.com); and Sylvia Menzies-Earl who so expertly and artfully formatted the pages for printing.

Others who made specific contributions are cited in footnotes.

DEDICATION

To:
Every warrior who went into combat on a one-way flight
—and the aircrews who flew them there.

FOREWORD

There are three ways to get light infantry inside an enemy perimeter by air—parachute, glider and airlift. We'll look at them all, but don't expect to see and read about every time silk deployed in the sky or a glider skidded to earth. We're going to look at the way airborne operations leaped into use early in the Second World War, matured through ever-larger units involved, from troops airlanded by transports through eleven gliders taking a modern fort in 1940, to a massive single lift of two airborne divisions at a single location screening the Rhine Crossing in 1945. We'll look at that growth, the mistakes, the successes and near successes of major operations, and touch on other examples where variations of airborne ops were tried. The main thread is ways and means of surprising an enemy with elite infantry on key ground to directly influence a battle.

This book doesn't follow what airborne troops did days and weeks after a landing. I'll tell no individual tales of shot and shell, blood and gore, leaving that to others who have experienced it, or 'historians' who think they understand it. Falling back on what I know, I look at military history and operations with different eyes. I want to show you pieces of the war with photos you probably haven't seen before, giving a new perspective. If you know my books, you know my forte is using Intelligence imagery, particularly aerial imagery for historical analysis. I consider aerial imagery a primary source on a par with official documents and first-hand accounts—it's just that most historians don't know how to use imagery properly. If the photo interpretation and combat analysis skills I bring to the task were good enough to report on current events and threats when I was on active duty, those techniques should serve to understand and interpret historic events from the same perspective. Just as for Intelligence Analysis during the Cold War or today, the only real limiting factor in historic imagery analysis is availability of source material.

Most of the imagery in this book came from two sources I had access to in the 1980s. All date from before or during the Second World War. Small scale vertical aerial photos are mainly from original roll negatives of Eighth and Ninth Air Force photoreconnaissance missions. Aerial obliques, some taken using hand-held 9" x 18" PR cameras, are Army Air Force public relations photos to document events (i.e., images with little or no Intelligence value to friendly forces). The rest of the photos, often indicated by a seven-digit 'accession number,' came from files of cut-negatives once held by US Army Air Force Intelligence or the Office of Naval Intelligence. Those photos often did have Intelligence value and came from American military attachés overseas, captured documents, briefings and military publications. A few of the cut-negs, ground and aerial shots came from British sources (all copied several times before reaching our files with associated loss in detail).

The negatives were each dutifully filed so they could be retrieved if needed again. But, by the time I screened the boxes filled with cut-negs, it had been years since their retrieval indexes with image pedigrees were destroyed. Fortunately I recognized a number of significant photos and kept copies.

The cut-negative files I reviewed were held by the Defense Intelligence Agency and serviced for all activities of the Department of Defense (DoD). I have no idea where they are today, or even if they still exist. I know many cans of original aerial film negatives, and a few boxes of cut-negs, went to the US National Archives & Records Administration (NARA) because I arranged the transfer. Disposition of the remainder of those cut film negatives is another story. With no index system they were not very useable. There was a lot of pressure to destroy those long dormant files to save storage cost. I'm just glad I had the wit to keep the copies I did so I could share them with you now. When you see a five to seven digit number in the lower corner of an image, it is an 'Accession Number' showing the original file location of a cut-neg. In the 1940s there were thousands of safes in the Pentagon basement holding tens of thousands of negatives for printing as required.

Some notes on mechanics of this book. Where possible aerial photos are oriented with north to the top of the page. Owners of my book *The Normandy Invasion* will recognize photos and text used again here. With so many wonderful photos in my possession I couldn't leave what 82nd, 101st and British 6th Airborne Divisions did on 6 June 1944 out of a book on airborne ops. I don't think it's plagiarism if you copy your own work. Some of my telling of Normandy airborne landings is corrected or refined in this book.

As I use it, the word airborne can refer to an operation, a technique/method, or a unit of parachute/glider infantry.

Both parachuting and gliding had roots going back to mythology—the primal urge to fly. Leonardo da Vinci had thoughts on both but both remained curiosities or stunts until the late nineteenth century. Gliding (heavier than air but without a motor) was but a precursor to powered flight. After the First First World War it was a sport.

Parachuting has roots back to Leonardo da Vinci but had no purpose until the First World War. Chutes were used to escape from Observation Balloons under attack from enemy fighter planes hoping to ignite their hydrogen filling. Few pilots used chutes until late in the war. No fighter pilot wanted to trade speed and altitude for the added weight. By the 1920s chutes were common in all types of aircraft and serious pilots, such as those carrying the mail, wouldn't fly without them (Charles Lindbergh jumped four times). 'Hitting the silk' was the standard remedy for the all too frequent engine failures, fires or structural failures. Parachutes were also used to drop supplies to beleaguered workers in crisis situation or disasters.

It wasn't until just before the Second World War that gliders and parachutes began to be thought of as weapons—tools for offense. That's where we begin. We shall follow that evolution to larger units, larger operations and larger missions.

Finally, the Second World War saw many uses of airborne techniques including combat landings, insertion of covert agents, Commando raids, and resupply of ground units in close combat. Some of those albeit important small-scale operations will be mentioned, but not covered in detail. We will follow the evolution of where and how well major airborne assaults got on the ground and accomplished their initial missions.

Chapter I

INTRODUCTION

No matter what the size or objective, an airborne assault is a daring offensive operation.[1] There were many small 'Special Ops' uses, such as extracting Mussolini from captivity in Campo Imperatore. The Japanese used paratroops three times and lost most in each try because of insufficient numbers committed (they also had gliders but never used them operationally). Italians dropped small contingents to destroy Allied aircraft in North Africa and the Soviets had at least two large drops. Most of those were side-shows involving small forces and not directly part of major campaigns. This book looks at the big drops/landings inserting infantry behind enemy lines in large numbers in an attempt change the initiative of a battle or campaign.

As usual in peacetime, the decades between the two World Wars saw senior officers concentrating on obtaining funding and their next promotion. Junior officers spent time training and thinking about how to do the job better. The more time they had, and fewer resources given them, the more thinking they did and the more radical the resulting ideas.

The Great Depression dried up resources, challenging military professionals to do more with less. When you have fewer troops, fewer guns, tanks and planes, husbanding them looms larger. You still have a job to do so you get creative.

Through the 1920s and 30s, military professionals all over the world reflected on the horrors of First World War trench warfare, minutely reexamining every battle, searching for a 'truth' that would avoid stalemate. Trench warfare was combat that ate men, destroying whole generations in England, France, Germany, Italy, and Russia with no appreciable gain for the price. Expecting war would come again, like any career professionals, military men considered their future. Haunted by the human wastage in 1914–18, they looked for new ways to resolve armed conflict. Soldiers had gone to ground in the face of ever more efficient rifles, machine guns and artillery. Trench lines, steadily more elaborate through the twentieth century, resulted in defenses that couldn't be outflanked and could only be broken by frontal assaults with losses so high they were no longer acceptable. Combat in Spain, China and Manchuria in the late 1930s quickly devolved into trench warfare. It looked like nothing had changed tactically. There had to be a better way.

The profession of arms is devoted to protecting a nation or winning any engagement where the nation decides armed force is required. Squandering your army on futile head-on attacks against defense positions housing machine guns and artillery doesn't serve either end, so an enormous amount of 'gray matter' was churning with imaginative planners advocating new (sometimes harebrained or impossible) ideas. Typically, 'Old Guard' upper ranks were wary, if not contemptuous, of 'newfangled' ways to fight.[2] The only consensus was that a modern military should be manned, equipped and use tactics designed to end battle quickly and decisively—no lengthy stalemates next time.

---

1. The only Second World War defensive uses of paratroops I know of were dropping 504th and 505th Parachute Infantry Regiments behind Allied lines to reinforce the Salerno, Italy beachhead on 13-14 September 1943 and a Soviet jump at Vyaz'ma, west of Moscow, on 27 January 1942.
2. My father, an Infantry Company Commander in the 1930s told me Regimental chalk-board problems often began, "You are on the Taneytown Pike…." That's Gettysburg!

This was a period of intense intellectual activity by retired and active duty officers seeking a magic bullet to negate the stagnation of trench warfare resulting in many ideas for tactics and equipment to avoid the horrific attrition of deadlocked trench warfare. Some of the ideas were sound and eventually came into use; others simply misspent scarce time and resources. Some advocates became zealots, writing convincingly in professional journals with passion and conviction that their vision was the right one. A few prophets gained followings. Armored vehicle pioneers Basil Liddell Hart, J.F.C. Fuller, Rommel and Charles de Gaulle pushed for larger, faster, better gunned tanks assuming the traditional role of cavalry or as a battering ram to open the door for regular infantry. In 1932 British PM Stanley Baldwin told Parliament, 'the bomber will always get through.' Airpower advocates like Italian General Giulio Douhet and US Army General Billy Mitchell pushed for what evolved into strategic bombing. Fighter pilots like Claire Chennault said 'no, the bomber would not get through.' The men who made big guns said they could make them bigger. In America and England, aging admirals argued the merits and relative value of big-gun warships while USN and RN 'Young Turks' held that aircraft carriers would own the seas. Expanding use of unrestricted submarine warfare was another popular concept in Germany. No one had the answers so everything was in play. Most of the new ideas were to improve the offense and most were steadily reined in by the Great Depression. Many of those ideas debated in Officer's Clubs and professional journals involved somehow exploiting the exciting and rapidly evolving technology of aviation.

European states that suffered the recent war on their soil, those with larger, bellicose neighbors, thought defensively. Philosophically led by men like Andre Maginot, France, Belgium and The Netherlands turned to modern designs of fortified defense lines facing Germany, barriers strong enough to deter or stop an aggressor at their borders (France also fortified its border with Italy). Thicker concrete and more steel was their hope. Even offensive-minded Germany followed suit with its Siegfried Line just east of the Rhine eventually reaching from Switzerland to the Netherlands.

You didn't have to halt an aggressor at the border, just delay them. Passive defenses were cheaper in men and material than actual armed bastions, and there was great pressure to remain within budgets a nation could afford. One of the most used passive defenses was belts of 'Dragon's Teeth'. They were 'state of the art' when a US military attaché forwarded this 1939 photo of German defenses. Concrete obstacles were relatively cheap to build and didn't require skilled labor. Their purpose was to block tanks and infantry; stalling them in fields-of-fire from strong-points and long-range heavy artillery as defense reinforcements moved forward.

1595633

Even more effective were elaborate belts of interlinked 'Elephant's Teeth,' another popular anti-tank defense (this installation is German from 1939). German photos are used here because US Army attachés in Berlin weren't collecting against an ally like France or Belgium, but a former enemy building up again was fair game.

1595632

Both sides used passive defenses extensively in lines that stretched for dozens of miles (as in this captured German photo of a slightly different French version).

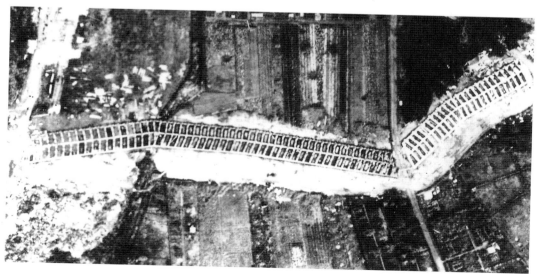

Proliferation of border fortresses and defense lines reinforced the 'offensivists' with proof that their search for new ways to advance was needed.

Military attachés of every nation forwarded to their Intelligence Services everything they could collect on defense lines as borders were being stiffened with wire and concrete. A few photos I screened came from covert collections but most were clipped from local magazines and newspapers (pre-Second World War security precautions and Intelligence collection were pretty naïve). The wire-lines below are very First World War in design. Steel tetrahedrons below were designed to stop tanks from breaking through. Similar 'Czech Hedgehogs' studded Normandy beaches in 1944. These passive defenses served to stall troops, making a killing zone for the armed strong-point in the distance.

1595630

11

95631

Soldiers constantly improved barbed wire entanglements and tank barriers that delineated borders but the real defensive power came from manned nodes (well-armed forts) backed by mobile heavy artillery farther to the rear. Fire-power was counted upon to deter an enemy from attacking or decimate him if he moved across the line.

1595628

Some of the forts were quite large. Others were merely outposts, not intended to stop an enemy, rather to act as a trip-wire. If that classic medieval approach failed, larger forts would at least stall an attacker. No offense could press deeper leaving such a threat in their rear. Forts were intended to hold an attacker in place so his force could be subjected to heavy, long range artillery fire, giving time for defending reserves to be mobilized and moved to oppose the threat. That deterrent was expected to make an attacker think twice—or keep him at bay while seriously damaging his offensive capability well short of a nation's heartland while defending troops remained safe behind steel and concrete.

This page from a German target study shows one gun of a French rail-gun battery supporting Maginot Line defenses from a location between Bitsch and Mutterhausen, threatening the area south of Pirmasens, Germany. The Germans used regular aerial photoreconnaissance beyond their borders to keep track of the locations of such guns.

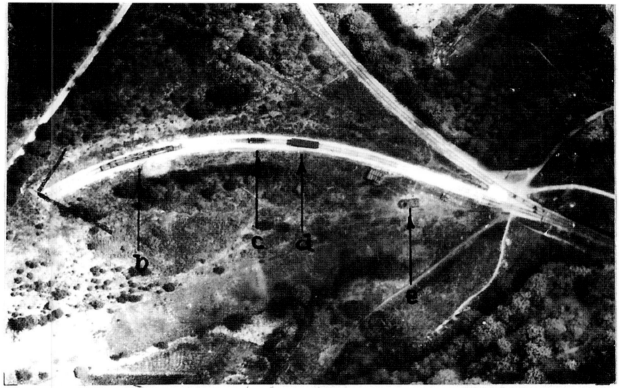

M etwa 1:2 800   Bild 2   Aufgen. 16.5
                                              1338

A large caliber, long range rail gun is at (b), a munitions car at (d), (c) is a car to move projectiles and propellants to the gun and a light anti-aircraft artillery position is at (e). This 16 May imagery is probably from 1938 when national tensions were high just before the German invasion of Poland. Germany was actively collecting excellent aerial photo intelligence about potential adversaries (Netherlands, Belgium, France and UK) using 'inadvertent' overflights of 'civilian aircraft' covertly equipped with cameras.

Enlargement of the French rail gun, probably 240mm or larger. Guns like this backed each fort or section of fortress line along the defense perimeter of the major nations.

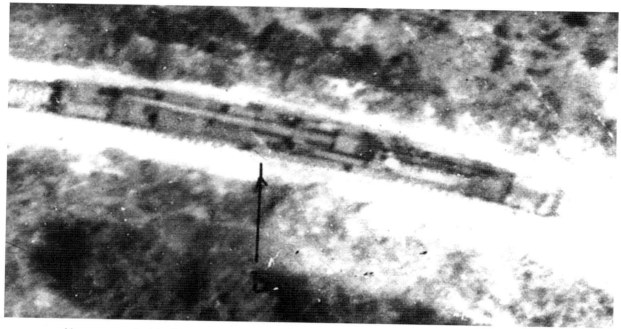

No one wanted to flail at formidable defenses and massed heavy artillery, but for some, rather than act as a deterrent, those powerful defenses stood as a challenge to more aggressive armies. Nations leaning toward offense rather than defense were the most active and imaginative in searching for ways to break through or sweep around lines of fortifications.

The concrete and steel defense school could fall back on a thousand years of development and design of forts, upgrading with modern materials, communications and weapons. No one on the other side of the argument could come up with a new tactic without new technology— new weapons or an entirely new approach. The ultimate weakness of the defense-minded solutions was the immutable truth that new weapons, more powerful weapons, more maneuverable weapons, could be devised and deployed faster than concrete and steel bunkers could be built and old forts upgraded.

Weapons of larger bore, higher velocity for better penetration, shaped charges and more efficient transport to support offensive tactics steadily improved through the 1920s and 30s, but the Depression kept funds limited. New technology is always expensive, so few of the new weapons were in general use—except in dictatorships. The budget 'guns vs. butter' debate was matched by 'cost vs. capability' debates resulting in a traditional bureaucratic response of going in ever decreasing concentric circles but it also stimulated even more imaginative solutions among frustrated soldiers.

One of the most inventive concepts involved an alliance between air-minded and infantry thinkers. Devoted and vocal advocates pushed for use of air-transport to defeat static defense lines by hopping riflemen over the Forward Edge of the Battle Area (FEBA) to attack an enemy from the rear. The idea was innovative and bold, stressing surprise and movement plus concentration of force at a soft spot. The weakness of this concept was limited load capacity of aircraft of the day. Limitations were rooted in the need for more powerful aircraft motors and lighter construction materials. Wood and fabric were too flimsy and steel too heavy. Fortunately

14

the infant airline industry all over the world was also pushing for faster planes with larger capacity and longer range; and aluminum was coming into use. Military theorists with few resources benefited from those commercial advances.

The Air Concept must be looked at as three different but related methods. Traditional land-force advocates pushed for ways to apply overwhelming numbers and technology to punch through a focal point (Schwerpunkt in German Doctrine) then pour fast moving mechanized forces through to totally circumvent or disrupt defensive schemes. Initially air advocates looked to achieve the same result with small numbers of elite troops inserted at key locations well behind massed defenders using transport planes, gliders or parachutes. There they counted on facing a less alert enemy spread thin and easily overwhelmed. Each of the variations of air movement attack depended upon tactical speed and surprise for success. Planners dreamed of massive airlifts but because of limited lift capacity, forces would only have light infantry weapons and large numbers of aircraft would be required (unlikely in Depression budgets). An alternative was multiple trips (necessitating short distances between launch base and objective and inviting ground-fire).

Each air-method was intended to take and control terrain by quickly capturing key points—bridges, airfields, ports, mountain passes or tunnels—taking them out of the defense network to curtail enemy movement, knocking an enemy off-balance, creating weakness. A corollary was capturing choke points, particularly bridges, to deny the enemy a chance to destroy them to impede one's own ground advance. Objectives taken by airborne assault would be held for a short time until conventional land forces could exploit the weaknesses created and advance to a link-up. None of the three methods were expected to be decisive by themselves; rather they were to be an important facet of a larger offensive. All three methods were utterly dependent upon quickly establishing and maintaining control of a landing ground/zone behind enemy lines with sufficient force to permit steady arrival of reinforcements and supplies until the link-up with on-coming land forces.

The first and most obvious airborne method was using transport planes to lift combat troops and light equipment, airlanding them at an enemy airdrome behind the main defenses (in those days any large, flat, unobstructed grass area would serve). This Trojan Horse-style attack presumes the chosen landing area to be undefended or lightly defended. A sudden infusion of superior numbers and weapons would take the field by storm, overwhelming any enemy present or nearby. The captured airhead would then be a base to fly in a steady stream of troops and expand into a major threat, pinching defending troops between air landed troops and oncoming armored and infantry divisions. The newly taken landing ground could also host fighter planes to control the airspace over the ad hoc battlefield.

Still with the same tactics and objectives, a second air concept had shock troops introduced behind enemy defenses by parachuting onto carefully selected targets. This required lengthy and expensive special training of the 'jumpers' but would be effective going into smaller landing zones and securing locations for subsequent airlanding. They could only deploy light weapons, but large or small numbers of soldiers could land in daylight or night and swiftly gather into effective combat units, taking advantage of surprise. The primary disadvantage was injury in landing and a potential for individual soldier landings being so scattered that surprise would be lost in the time it took for troops to assemble.

Small aircraft payload was also a problem for this concept. Other limits to the effectiveness of parachute insertion were weather, ground obstacles, ground opposition and the skill and courage of the airlift pilots. Because of rigorous physical training, risk of a jump and mission to fight alone until relieved, paratroopers quickly came to think of themselves as an elite force—and indeed many of them were.

Italy was the first to test a large drop. It was in 1927 and didn't result in creation of a major airborne force.

One of the earliest successful parachute-troop platforms was an obsolete (1930) four-engined Soviet bomber with open cockpits for pilots and gunners.

The early '30s Soviet Tupolev TB-3, carried one of the largest loads with 35 men, but they jumped in a primitive and dangerous manner, exiting on the top of the fuselage, standing on the wing and jumping in turn as shown in this German Intelligence Study. That meant they had to jump with little equipment. One of the largest aircraft of its day, airspeed just over 100 mph made the TB-3 extremely vulnerable to enemy fighters, rendering them useless as bombers. But the Soviets had a lot of the ponderous planes so they were used in the war with Finland, for homeland defense, and airlanding supplies after the German Invasion in June 1941.

American military attachés reported Soviet troops untrained in parachute jumping actually diving off of low and slow flying TB-3s into deep snow without using chutes. The injury rate was high, but desperately needed troops were delivered near or behind on-coming German lines. It sounds like something Stalin would condone.

A third airborne concept, using the same logic as above, sought to overcome the limitations of airlift capacity and numbers by augmenting the available lift with disposable gliders to increase the lift-size. Gliders were cheap to build, pilots cheap to train, and the infantry transported didn't require special training. Obsolescent aircraft used as tugs could make a glider trip and return to base to pick up another load, thus expanding the overall lift capacity. Only Nazi Germany had forces trained and equipped for all three airborne delivery methods when the Second World War began. Britain and America established their airborne capabilities after being impressed by German successes.

All three methods were used in various combinations during the Second World War, the first being Airlift/Airlanding.

While alternatives for rapidly moving troops long distances using aircraft were explored by many nations during the 1930s, the concepts were sound but aircraft weren't yet up to the task. In 1930, rugged and reliable Ford tri-motor planes could only carry ten passengers. The Germans got into the airborne business early. Their most numerous transport plane of the era was the tri-motor Junkers Ju 52. Beginning as a civil transport in 1932, it cruised at 100mph (top speed 121mph), could climb to 11,000 feet, had a 620 mile range and could carry 18 troops (a German rifle company in 1940 was 90 men, so five aircraft). Variously called 'Tante Annie' (Auntie Annie), 'Iron Annie' or 'Tante Ju' the Junkers transport was found in large numbers where ever the German Army went.

Below, some aircraft had a wide cargo door on the right. Mobilizer wheels are being taken away from a 2cm Flak 30 about to be loaded.

The Ju 52's cramped interior and a personnel small door on the left side limited gear a jumper could carry and meant slow exit on a jump. That meant troops scattered on landing resulting in slow assembly.

Below is an example. This is a German jump in the Balkans in 1941. Looks like they jumped pretty high. The sticks from eight planes are coming down loose.

For comparison, Britain, which didn't have airborne units in 1940, had three companies in a battalion (about 40 men each so two DC-2s). Moving a regiment would require commitment of a lot of planes, a lot of crews, a lot of maintenance. Clearly the air-oriented thinkers needed larger planes. Fortunately technology was moving fast.

The next step in aviation was the 1000-mile range 14-passenger twin-engine American Douglas DC-2 in 1934. A year later Douglas came out with the legendary DC-3/C-47 Skytrain/Dakota with a range of 1,500 miles. One of the greatest aircraft of the war, the revolutionary new plane had retractable landing gear and cruised at 160 mph with a top speed of 224. It carried twenty-eight troops and their equipment and the planes could be modified to transport animals, light artillery pieces and surprisingly large loads of supplies.

British 1st Airborne Division troopers on the way to Arnhem show the greater room for people and gear in a Dakota. There is also an aisle to permit movement in the air and lining up for a jump. A large personnel door on the left made exits faster. The jump door could be widened to a cargo door that would accept a Jeep or light artillery gun.

Other planes, such as the 62 passenger Curtiss-Wright C-46 'Commando' and Messerschmitt Me 323[3] which could carry 130 troops 500 miles were introduced later in the war, but the Ju 52 and C-47 proved to be the workhorse aircraft of the Second World War and no Army ever had enough of them to satisfy the myriad competing demands.

When war began, there were few air-transportable vehicles and artillery pieces, or aircraft with sufficient door width to carry them. This severely limited what airborne combat operations might accomplish in a few days before heavier defense forces could be marshaled against the lighter airborne infantry as at Arnhem.

While landing at airfields (obvious locations) couldn't produce the same degree of surprise as 'jumpers' or glider landed infantry, air landing using transport planes could quickly move a lot of troops and equipment to a critical point with multiple shuttle lifts.[4] Transport airlanding was successful IF a landing ground could be swiftly occupied and secured (a good task for jumpers). However, to be decisive, a lot of aircraft (or multiple trips) were required. That meant either a huge number of planes had to be assembled, potentially giving away the surprise, or flight distances had to be short enough to permit many fast turn-around trips.

The first combat airlift occurred when shuttle flights of 25 Luftwaffe Ju 52s transports carried 15,000 of Franco's troops, several batteries of artillery and their supplies from Morocco to Spain between 29 July and 11 October 1936—helping decide the Spanish Civil War. That success encouraged German planners to keep the technique in their play book but they didn't factor in the lack of air and ground opposition to the Spanish airlift when assessing the results.

Of course transports used for airlift might be on a one-way flight unless the landing field was firmly in control and defended.

GLIDERS

Gliders proved an attractive air assault option to planners who didn't have to ride them in. They required tow-planes, many of which were the same transport planes that were constantly in demand for other applications, including parachuting and airlift. Risk was minimized for tow-planes because gliders could be cut loose outside weapons range at a well-defended target. Of more significance, a glider LZ had to be a broad, flat open area (many times larger than a parachute drop zone). An LZ had to be well marked and easily identified because a glider pilot had only ONE chance to get down safely. A glider landing on unsecured ground was extremely risky because the troops were highly vulnerable to enemy ground fire during landing and getting out of the glider. Experience quickly demonstrated that night landing of gliders was a particularly dicey proposition—LZ identification, depth perception of altitude and avoiding other gliders already on the ground were just some of the difficulties.

Germany came to glider warfare early and naturally. Denied most powered flight by the treaty ending the First World War, thousands of German pilots got flight experience by gliding (and secretly going to then ally, the Soviet Union, to train on powered flight). 'Private' glider clubs sprang up all over Germany and were very popular in the 1920s and 30s.

Germany's most numerous military glider was the *Deutsche Forschungsanstalt für Segelflug* (DFS) 230. First flown in 1933, it carried ten men (a pilot and nine soldiers) and could only carry troops. One of the first US looks was a much copied photo of a DFS 230 from a US Army Attaché Report from Berlin before America was in the war. The photo below was probably from an 'open source' such as a German newspaper or magazine. Date and location of the photo are unknown, but certainly before 1941. At this time neither the British nor Americans had an operational military glider program.

---

3. A Me 321 'Gigant' glider powered with six captured French radial engines. They were used in the USSR and the Mediterranean for resupply, not air-assault.
4. The modern inheritor of this tactic uses helicopters, technology not available in the Second World War.

This photo of a DFS 230 forwarded by an attaché before the war couldn't provide much Intelligence on the plane or its capacity, beyond the skid indicating a short landing distance. It was enough to whet the appetites of planners in other countries.

No matter what the glider, its initial purpose was to carry infantry, their equipment and supplies behind enemy lines. Later in the war when resupply problems became critical and transport aircraft were insufficient, large German gliders were enlisted to move reinforcements and material to forces engaged in North Africa and The Soviet Union.

More is known about the next photo. Also in a US Army Attaché Report this one had to come from a neutral capitol. It shows three Ju 87s towing three DFS 230 gliders at Kjevik, the airport for Kristiansand, Norway, on 1 October 1943. It too was obviously from a German source. It is unclear why the Germans needed gliders in Occupied Norway, or how they might be used. Hitler's paranoia kept large forces in Norway to the end of the war—troops and planes that might have been better used elsewhere.

The most significant information from this photo was that the relatively light glider could be pulled by a single-engine tug. In this case Ju 87 'Stukas,' which were obsolescent in Western European air by 1942, and in good supply, thus saving precious Ju 52s for other work.

The heavier (4,000 lbs.) American-built Weaver Aircraft Company CG-4A 'Waco' (British 'Hadrian') carried two pilots and thirteen troops and their equipment. The nose hinged up, providing a large opening, so a Waco could carry a Jeep, light artillery piece or bulk supplies. The wing and center of gravity were well forward so the glider could 'nose over' and was occasionally seen flipped onto its back. Light (flimsy) construction of gliders made any cargo they carried like a loose cannon on the deck in a crash or rough landing.

Most images found in the collection of Intelligence files I was screening were negatives. The one below was a print. A typed caption glued on the back read, 'NIGHT FLYING—Glider pilots, taught night flying, learn to land their motorless aircraft on pin-point destinations night or day. Night operations have proven to be a decided advantage over the enemy. Notice the giant C-47 Troop Carrier in the background.'

The caption suggests it is from an exercise someplace in North Carolina early in 1943 (before American gliders were actually used operationally and night landings were proven unwise). I particularly enjoyed the delightful naïveté of 'giant C-47.'

The photo shows non-retractable wheels and skids. Made of fabric covered wood and metal framework, sixteen small companies had delivered 13,900 Wacos to American and British airborne units by the end of the war. It was the principal American glider and was occasionally used by the British.

Waco wasn't a great vehicle but it was good enough. Lightly constructed it was built easy and fast so large numbers were available and, in a military operation the rule is often 'quantity is quality…if you've got enough.'

The only night glider landings in combat that came out well were Eben Emael and British landings in Normandy.

Glider training in the US began in earnest in August 1942. This photo is probably typical of pilot training exercises. It is Field Number 3 in North Carolina on 25 September 1944. Seventy Wacos got down successfully. They are tightly grouped and nicely aligned in the same direction…and nobody flipped over. Of course this was an unopposed daylight landing on a flat, open, unobstructed LZ. The photo illustrates the large area required for landing a little over 900 troops.

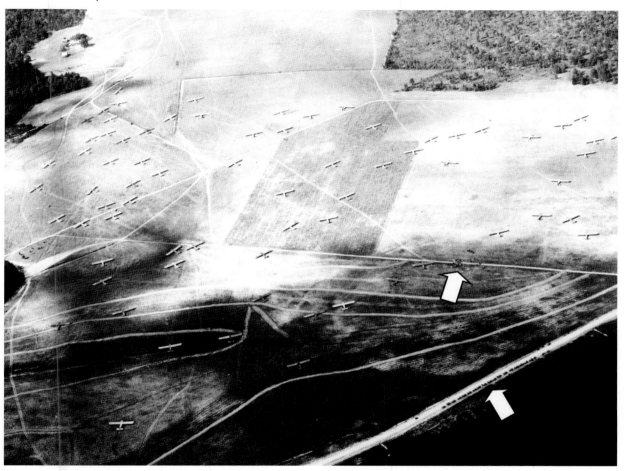

Eighteen trucks and ten smaller vehicles (some staff cars) are waiting on the road (lower arrow) to take participants back to base, suggesting no Parachute Infantry were involved.

The upper arrow points to a cluster of men and vehicles on the interior road. If that is a crashed glider it is more destroyed than any I saw in combat imagery. The only possible glider parts are a possible left wing and the tail. I can't see it well enough to tell what is going on.

The 8,300 lb. British Airspeed Ltd. AS.51 'Horsa' needed a longer landing run than the Waco. It was Britain's most used glider and the best glider in the war. Developed in 1941, Horsa could carry 25-30 infantry. This photo was sent me by a friend and is one of the few images in the book not from retired Intelligence files I screened. Possibly from an operational landing, the photo shows the relatively steep descent angle typically used to drive a glider in a 'carrier landing' on the chosen landing ground. This glider was used by both UK and US forces. Almost under the Horsa wheels is a probable 'Hamilcar' glider.

Troops exited a Horsa by doors on each side. To unload larger cargos such as vehicles or trailers, the tail could be removed. Below are two Horsas west of Arnhem, illustrating a difference in paint jobs. The one on the left still wears Normandy Invasion recognition stripes.

Replacement for Germany's DFS 230 was the Gotha Go 242, seen in an Allied Intelligence drawing from 1942. Introduced in 1941, the Gotha carried up to 23 troops or comparable cargo load. Like the other gliders it made use of fabric over a light metal frame. Skids made for shorter landings. The Allied artist didn't know the Gotha also had wheels.

LIFT SPOILERS OPEN

FORWARD SKID RETRACTED

HR.

CONFIDENTIAL

Go 242
A·1·2 (G)

I.D. 2591

Below, the file caption said two Gothas in train were being towed by a single Bf 110 (off the left side of the photo). I doubt it. My guess is the photo was taken from the open dorsal gun position in the left fuselage of a He 111z which was the actual tow-plane.

A 10 July 1943 photo of Olmütz Airdrome, 45 miles northeast of Brno in eastern Czechoslovakia, shows 45 twin-boom Go 242 gliders lined up on the ramp. Aircraft parking arrangement and the presence of 12 light planes (some of them bi-planes) suggests a glider pilot training base. I believe the Go 242 was only used for resupply in the Med.

On grass at the top are 19 single-engine aircraft with a decidedly Junkers-looking wing—perhaps Junkers W 34s used as tugs for the lightly loaded gliders.

DSF 230, Go 242, Waco and Horsa were produced in large numbers and made up the bulk of equipment used in airborne operations during the Second World War. After 1943, German use of gliders was mainly for supply of troops in combat zones.

Necessity being the mother of rearmament, Germany was ahead of the Allies in large gliders. By 1942, losses and demands on the Ju 52 fleet to resupply troops in North Africa and the Soviet Union demonstrated the need of a heavy hauler that was cheap. The Messerschmitt Me 321 glider was the result.

First seen in 1941, the 'Gigant' had a wingspan of 180.5 feet (77 feet more than a B-17). It could carry a medium tank, an 88mm gun and prime-mover, or 130 troops with combat equipment.

The problem was, loaded it weighed 37 tons so a lot of horsepower was required to get one into the air. Trying to use planes being pushed out of front-line service, such as the Bf 110, a complicated lash-up using three 'Zerstorers' was devised. They could get a 'Gigant' into the air, but a lot of take-off accidents resulted from tow-cables pulling the aircraft together as they took the load. One solution was splicing two aging He 111 bombers together to make a twin fuselage, five motor aircraft, the He 111Z. That plane was only used as a tug for Me 321s.

Right is a Me 321 towed by a 'troika' of Bf 110s during an exercise apparently involving a para-drop.

A more workable solution was installing engines on the Me 321 to make the Me 323. The first versions used six motors captured during the invasion of France to power each glider conversion.

Below is an RAF photo of the Messerschmitt Factory at Regensburg, Germany on 3 April 1943. It shows six of the powered Messerschmitt 'Gigants' (Me 323), four Me 321 gliders (two incomplete) and one He 111z tow-plane. Almost every aerial photo I've seen of groups of Me 321s, at least one will be minus a tail. They nose-loaded, so perhaps tail damage was common.

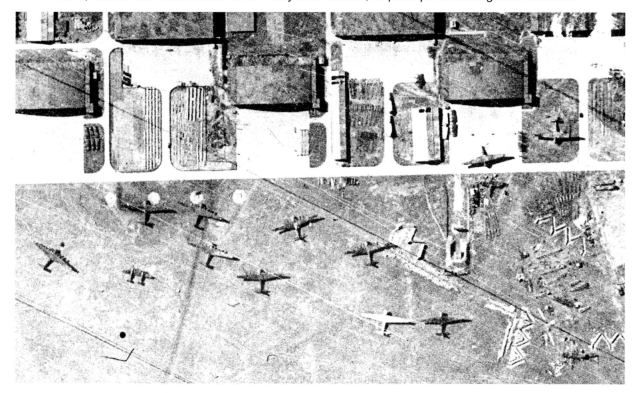

British Hamilcar GAL. 49, made by General Aircraft Ltd., answered the Me 321. Though smaller, it could carry a light tank or two Bren Gun Carriers. They weren't used until 1944 in Operations Overlord, Market Garden and Varsity, and only in small numbers.

Large non-retractable wheels made for good rough-surface landings. A single pilot cockpit atop the square cross-section fuselage permitted good visibility and allowed heavy loads and a clear opening of the entire interior space. Exit was through side doors or the detachable nose.

PARACHUTE INFANTRY

Mention airborne and most people think parachutists, the elite of the trade. Once again Germany led the way, using 'jumpers' in combat two years before the British and Americans began airborne unit training.

These *Fallschirmjäger* wear the distinctive airborne helmet and many carry sub-machineguns. We can see their reserve chutes. Note the small exit door which also limited drop of bulk supplies and heavier or larger equipment such as anti-tank guns or light howitzers. That is an open-air M/G position on the top of the Ju 52.

Below is a German photo of a three-ship formation showing paratroops exiting Ju 52s. Spacing between jumpers doesn't indicate the urgency of a combat jump (note the 'swan dive' from the man jumping from the background plane), nor are any arms or other combat equipment in evidence. This was probably a photo of training acquired by an American military attaché in Berlin, which dates it prior to 1942.

Another probable German public relations photo catches the jump sequence from exiting the Ju 52 door to opening the chute. It likely reached the US in an attaché report. It appears these jumpers weren't using static lines to open chutes as did the Americans and British paratroops. Absence of other planes, a view from almost directly underneath, and apparent absence of combat gear, suggests this may also be from a training exercise or public demonstration. Before the US entered the Second World War, our attachés were still able to pick up material in Berlin. Note the jump sequence is tighter than in the photo above.

The accession number of this photo (ID 3310) is one ahead of the photo below, so they likely arrived in Washington at the same time.

Clearly from an 'open source,' (bleed-through indicates a newspaper), collected by a US military attaché in Berlin before America entered the war. Photos like this gave Allied Intelligence something to 'chew on'. I eventually learned it was a propaganda photo from the April 1940 Invasion of Norway.

I.D. 3311

32

All three air-transport means of inserting troops in a battle are essentially offensive and Germany was primarily on the defensive from 1943 on with their airborne troops fighting as 'Leg Infantry'. By 1943 the Germans had apparently forgotten, or had no opportunity to relive, the lessons of truly brilliant 'surgical use' of small forces of paratroops and gliders early in the war. Even the occurrence of foreign-source (Third Party) negatives covering airborne ops began to dry up in US Intelligence Files.

The fourth essential element in airborne operations is aircrew of tow and/or jump aircraft who could grit their teeth and hold a cumbersome, wet-wing plane straight and level through what could be intense flak and automatic weapons fire. An airborne op was like a bombing approach, only much lower and slower (hopefully over a less defended location). Day or night, despite weather and enemy resistance, transport aircrew had to correctly navigate to find Landing Zones (LZ) and Drop Zones (DZ), then deliver their troops on target. They had to hold to precise altitudes and airspeeds to let paratroops safely jump or gliders drop tow-cables.

Some authors have maligned troop carrier crews on certain Allied airborne ops as poorly trained and motivated. Unfortunately most 'historians' have never been in uniform, much less near combat.

True, many of the transport pilots had little 'stick time'[5] and few had any combat experience—but getting shot at accelerates the learning curve. Also true, some transport aircrew couldn't do the job, or did it poorly, but hundreds of German, British and American pilots and crews faced the music and faithfully took their loads to the heart of the dance at the risk of their own lives. Several airborne landings have examples of aircrew sacrificing themselves, holding steady on target with their plane on fire and going down, giving paratroops a chance to jump. Those who provided the 'borne' in airborne must not be demeaned or forgotten.

Considering all the elements of airborne operations, no matter the method of delivery, the keys are—SURPRISE, SPEED and FOCUS. The name of the game was get light infantry in fast and clean, take the objective(s) and hold the ground until reinforced or relieved.

Let's see how the warring nations met the challenge.

---

5. Actually 'wheel time' given the controls of most transport aircraft. A lot of those pilots migrated into my chosen career field when they weren't needed in cockpits. As a junior officer I heard their stories during coffee breaks and Squadron parties.

Chapter II

FIRST USE – 1940

NORWAY

Occupation of Norway was thought essential to protect Germany's northern flank, access to the North Atlantic, and critical sources of iron ore and fish oil. Geography and terrain made Blitzkrieg based on mechanized forces out of the question and several key locations on the 800 mile length of the country had to fall almost simultaneously. There was no land route between German forces and Norway so sea and air had to be used. First day control of airfields was vital, so Nazi planning fell back on their Spanish Civil War experience but the heavy lifter was going to be troop carrier planes bring in ground troops.

Number of paratroops used was small but the Germans were writing Airborne Doctrine and everyone else was watching.

I didn't find much on Norway in US Intelligence files until attention turned to the Heavy Water Plant at Rjukan (see my book *V-Weapons Hunt*), and all of that material was from British sources.

This RAF photo is Stavanger airdrome during the German invasion of Norway (9 April-10 June 1940). There are ten Ju 52s and four Ju 88s on the field.

Two of the 'Tante Ju' aircraft have pranged into each other, and shadows under a Ju 88 at center right suggest its right landing gear has collapsed.

Below, German paratroops landing at Narvik in far northern Norway. The force was small but faced little resistance and quickly intimidated local defenders. Most drops in Norway were battalion-size.

Infantry disgorging from transport aircraft quickly gained control over airfields, making possible a fly-in of more troops and fighter planes.

Relatively few transport planes were involved but the attack worked, largely because of complete surprise and light air and ground opposition. Quick capture of Norwegian airfields allowed short-range, high-performance Luftwaffe fighters to dominate the air, aiding German forces to quickly outnumber and defeat weak British attempts to create bridgeheads opposing the invasion. Of the 70 Ju 52s lost, only five were lost to combat (RAF bombing), the rest were operational losses (crash landings and collisions). High density air traffic into small or underdeveloped landing grounds, repeated shuttle flights with only emergency maintenance, and tired, stressed aircrew proved to be a prescription for accidents.

This undated RAF photo is Trondheim-Vaernes Air Drome (A/D), during the invasion. Copied through several generations, increasing contrast and losing detail, making counts and ID of aircraft difficult, but I make 94 planes around the landing area, 50 of them Ju 52s.

Forces invading Norway (and Denmark) would have to solidify control before France or Britain could intervene and, because the date for invasion of the Low Countries was nearing, all available aircraft were employed to overwhelm Norway. Most of the German Navy was also involved hauling or supporting ground forces. Other German troops spilled out of merchant ships 'innocently' arriving in ports from Copenhagen to Narvik. The Norwegians had a force nearly as large as Germany used, and they put up quite a fight, but without the best weapons, and many troops immobile in forts, the issue was never really in doubt. Germany lost nearly 6,000 casualties, 110 aircraft, one heavy and two light cruisers, ten destroyers and six submarines.

A-12-NORWAY-(TRONDHEIM-VAERNES A/D)-NO.520 PHOTO TAKEN
1670.410

670410

Enlargement also discloses a number of small single-engine aircraft on the ground. I count ten at lower left. Those fighters doomed British intervention.

German invasions of Denmark and Norway began on 9 April 1940. British intervention was too little, too late and too far from logistical support to succeed. The Danes surrendered in two hours and a puppet government was quickly installed in Norway, but fighting ceased only after 62 days of resistance.

Jumpers were effective in Norway, quickly taking control of key positions. This is a better version of a photo used in Chapter I.

INVASION OF THE WEST

Western Allies reacted to the loss of Norway and Denmark by accelerating mobilization and moving troops toward the German border. French and British forces could take away the German advantage in numbers, potentially resulting in a First World War stalemate. Hitler knew time wasn't on his side. He had to get past the border barriers quickly so, 32 days after the Invasion of Norway, Germany executed 'Fall Gelb' (Case Yellow), Invasion of The Netherlands, Belgium and France. The concept was to draw Allied forces north, away from their bases and prepared positions, then knife in behind them with a powerful armored strike through the supposedly impassable Ardennes Forest. Meticulous planning and aerial reconnaissance identified bridges and airfields near Rotterdam essential to swift advances into southern Holland and northern Belgium and German paratroops were assigned the task of securing those objectives. Paratroop units were not fully up to strength again but time was critical. Objectives were key line-of-communication points and airfields so airlift could bring in reinforcements until relieved by the massive armored and heavy armed ground force closing rapidly from less than 50 miles away.

Fallschirmjäger (parachute hunters, i.e., light infantry) were highly effective and caught the attention of strategists in Britain and America. Serious Allied interest in airborne capability dates from German operations during Fall Gelb.

Glider and parachute infantry secured other key bridges ahead of the German advance during invasion of the Netherlands. A Dutch trader on his way north to Rotterdam early morning on 10 May 1940 found himself in the middle of one of the German drop zones as paratroops landed to secure bridges across the big rivers in western Holland. The trader had the courage to use his camera, capturing these photos of Ju 52s and *Fallschirmjäger* coming down near the Moerdijk bridges over Holland's Diep, 14 miles south of Rotterdam.[6]

A flight of three Ju 52s starting to unload parachute infantry. These operations were mainly regimental-size.

6. I am indebted to Pastor F.G Thuring of Groesbeek, Netherlands, who sent me the booklet containing these photos in 1980.

As far as I know these are the first photos of paratroops in a combat landing. The photographer was fortunate it was early in the war and soldiers were still considerate of non-combatants.

There seems to be little urgency in troops moving to assemble. It's clear this landing was unopposed. Elsewhere, alerted by events in Norway, Dutch soldiers were better prepared and put up resistance that took the Germans by surprise.

7th Flieger Division
Later, 1st Fallschirmjäger Div

German photo of paratroops jumping at Rotterdam.

German advances in the spring of 1940 provided more military propaganda than tactical advantage, giving the entire Wehrmacht an unwarranted aura of invincibility, but at the time the fear they engendered in units of traditional foot soldiers can't be overstated (those guys jump out of perfectly good airplanes—they're crazy). Tactical radio communication was primitive and cumbersome in 1940, thus troops on both sides had a hard time just knowing what was happening around them. As in Poland, unseasoned troops were susceptible to confusion and panic while the attackers (often just as unseasoned) had the confidence of winning ground and knowing where they were going. To the Dutch and Belgians (and later the French and British), it seemed like the German paratroops were everywhere, and impossible to stop. Once defenders started to retreat before the German Army there was no good place to regroup and fight with confidence, and the speeding German ground spearheads always seemed to be one jump ahead.

However, ground fire by determined Dutch defenders made a shambles of at least one joint parachute and airlift landing—an omen for future similar operations. The Luftwaffe retaliated by completely destroying sections of Rotterdam.

America was a non-belligerent so its military attachés had remarkable access to the German advance and were significantly impressed. The most dramatic coup was assault neutralization of Belgian Fort Eben Emael that began the Invasion of Belgium.

Losses in Norway had been a shock and the Wehrmacht didn't want to begin war in the West squandering strength in frontal assaults on the heavy guns and heavy fortifications of the much vaunted Maginot Line. That well-known and superficially impressive line of French fortifications ran from the Swiss border to the Ardennes.

France depended upon her ally Belgium to defend her northern border. Belgian forts facing Germany were not as massive as the Maginot forts, not so much a line as a series of strong points intended to delay an attacker for roughly five days—until reinforcements could be brought up. German planners rightly estimated that few of those national troops would continue to fight after the surrender of their governments, but a powerful modern fort with large caliber guns sitting on the German attack route could not be brushed aside or ignored.

The German plan was to take the Low Countries out of the war quickly by striking where French and Belgian defense lines met, crossing the Meuse (Maas) River west of Maastricht, and driving armored columns behind the advancing Allied front.

Fort Eben Emael, on the west side of the Albert Canal two miles south of Maastricht and six miles north of Lüttich (Liège), was the hinge on the door the Germans intended to throw open for their armored sweep behind Allied infantry plodding north to meet the more traditional, and more expected, sweeping German advance into the Low Countries.

FORT EBEN EMAEL

Most of the images that follow are from a meticulous German Intelligence study of the fort. This graphic shows the location of the fort at the confluence of the Maas River and Albert Canal. It was roughly triangular with 40 meter-high near vertical walls. The fort was manned by 1200 troops and had plenty of concrete and steel armored firing positions for howitzers, anti-tank guns and machine guns. The biggest threat to German troops crossing three Maas bridges to the north or south were twin 120mm guns in a steel turret that presented a low profile to enemy artillery.

White dots running north and northwest from the fort along the canal and road are strongpoints of lesser than fort status, usually defended with light artillery and machine guns. Belgium is to the lower left, the Netherlands up and west of the river. Germany is fifteen miles straight east.

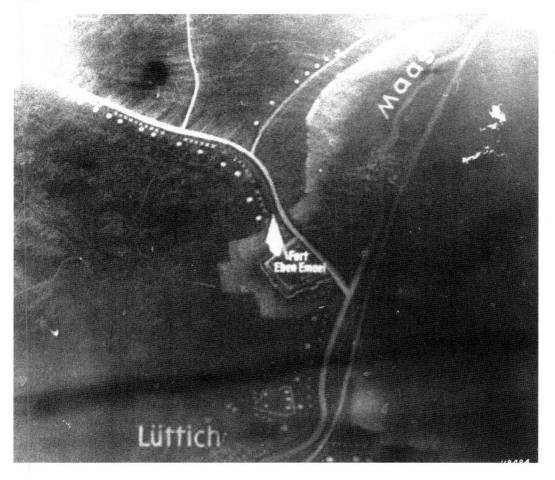

*Artillerie – Panzerturm,
wie in der Mitte der Anlage*

This is the five-meter diameter armored turret in the center of the fort. It mounted the heaviest guns in Eben Emael. Clearly there is one 120mm gun showing but ground truth says the turret mounted two, so this may be an early version, or representative rather than the actual main turret in Eben Emael.

The fort was new, completed in 1935, incorporating all the latest technology and design. Defenders were billeted nearby and rotated into the fort weekly. Roughly 600 to 650 defenders could be expected inside the fort at any time. Eben Emael was built with plenty of concrete and steel armored firing positions; including 75mm guns in armored turrets (cupolas-'Kuppel') much like on a warship. There were sixteen 75mm, four of them in three-meter diameter double turrets, at least twelve 60mm anti-tank weapons positioned for horizontal fire to sweep the walls, and 11 positions with some 30 machine-guns. At least two of those positions were designed to control the open space inside (atop) the fort.

On paper Eben Emael looked formidable—it just happened that the whole concept of relying on large static defensive positions was in the process of being made obsolete by technical improvements in munitions, the airplane and fast-moving armored units. Of course, few in France and Belgium saw this truth in 1939–40 but a few days in May and June were going to make it quite obvious to anyone who'd pay attention.

The futility of staking defense hopes on static positions is shown in this photo of the effect of high-velocity 88mm anti-aircraft guns firing horizontally at Belgian Fort Nef Chateau's armored cupolas. A more traditional shape with firing windows and topped by a periscope, this steel turret was based upon First World War experience. Nef Chateau (or Neufchateau) defended Liege and was overrun early in the German advance west. This photo was taken on 1 June 1940 by a US military attaché accompanying advancing German forces as an observer.

Another photo from Nef Chateau on 1 June shows reinforced concrete bunkers after repeated direct fire from 88mm anti-aircraft guns. The German Army permitted attachés from non-belligerent nations to examine the results. An American officer is fourth from the left and another third from the left in the center group.

Evidence from Poland in 1939 that keeping the casemates and armored cupolas smothered with local fire and bringing up heavy artillery to fire at near-point-blank ranges would soon reduce a fort to impotency. But Eben Emael's casemates were immune to direct fire from outside the fort. They were designed to sweep the perimeter and top of the fort with artillery and automatic weapons fire[7].

Most of the photos in this sub-chapter are from before the German invasion of Belgium. This is one of Eben Emael's concrete casemates. Eben Emael had four of these each containing three 75mm guns (German PIs thought it was five). Fresh dirt and no guns in evidence suggest the photo was taken during or shortly after construction. It may have been taken covertly by German contractors working on the fort. It is more likely from an 'open source' such as a Belgian magazine or newspaper circa 1936 or 1937. I was unable to match this casemate with ground detail, particularly the background buildings on higher ground, which makes me suspect this may be from another similar Belgian fort and used in the German Eben Emael target study as an example of typical (or identical) defenses to be encountered.

Artillerie - Flankierungswerk

---

7. Automatic weapons are usually rifle caliber (.30 or .50) up to 20mm, with a high rate of continuous fire. Useful against ground and air attack, they pose a real threat to aircraft up to 3,500-4,000 feet (i.e., well covering parachute jump and glider approach altitudes).

The Albert Canal was cut through a hill to keep it in Belgian territory, creating a gorge and angle with the Maas that was ideal for positioning a fort.

The fort was atop canal walls like these, making direct fire on the casemates from the east bank impossible and land assault directly across the canal extremely expensive.

AREA 12---BELGIUM---VIEW OF THE CROHENHOVEN CUT OF THE ALBERT CANAL BETWEEN ANTWERP AND LIEGE--- PHOTO TAKEN PRIOR TO MAY, 1940.
                                                                    ISC #176

Small-scale aerial imagery from the German Target Study shows Eben Emael dominating higher ground overlooking the Albert Canal locks, nearby Maas River and three bridges (at least one of significant size). The photo was probably taken in 1939 using a German mapping camera (individual frames were 11.9" square) mounted in a Luftwaffe plane disguised as a Lufthansa airliner. Similar covert imagery collection missions were occurring over Dutch, Belgian, French and English Channel Ports.

The fort is just north of where the Albert Canal splits off to the northwest.

The circle at upper right is a clock, typical of German imagery of the period. Bottom right is a frame counter, in this case frame number 077 on the roll of film.

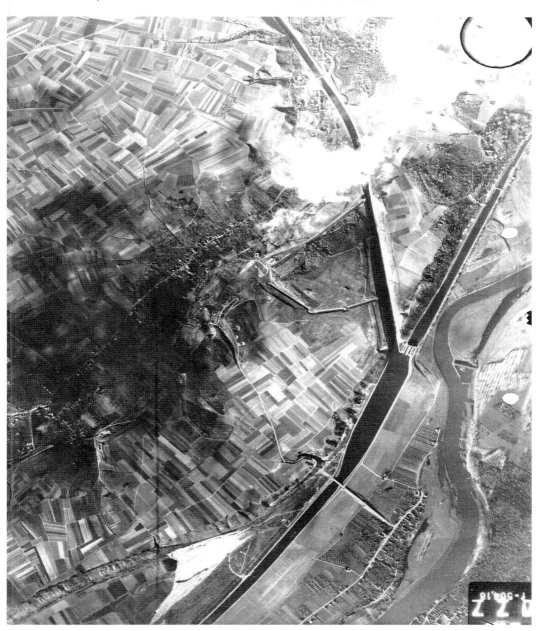

A German photo taken on a later date (note new paths and five vehicles on the road in front of the main entrance to the fort—center left—that weren't on the photo above), large-scale imagery (probably from early 1940) permitted a forensic analysis of the facility, resulting in the target overlay that follows. This imagery was undoubtedly used in planning the German attack on the fort.

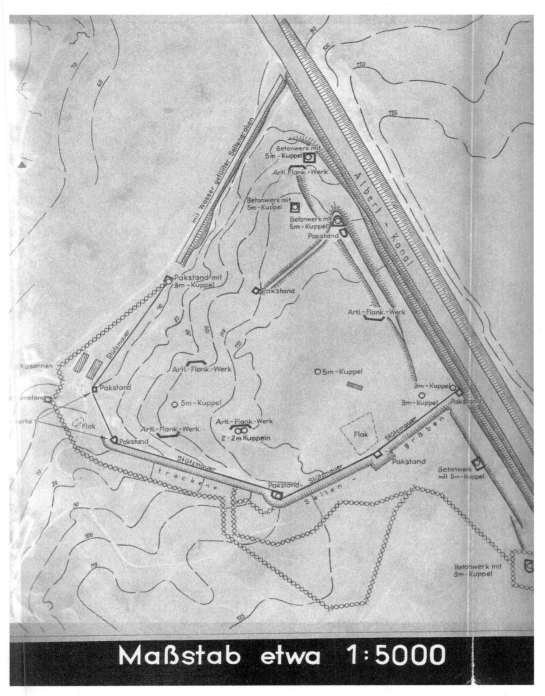

Maßstab etwa 1:5000

Detailed German Army PI work identified twelve 'Kuppel,' armored turrets (5m, 3m and 2m in diameter); five field artillery positions; locations for flak; nine wall-positions for the anti-tank guns; and two outlier-bastions south along the canal, beyond the walls of the fort proper. It also shows extensive barbed-wire lines, making it clear that assaulting the fort from the ground would be costly. The five meter diameter turret at fort center mounted 120mm howitzers that were the greatest threat to a German advance.

Map scale is given as 1:5000. Elevations are shown in five meter contour lines.

Denied even covert access to Fort Eben Emael, German Intelligence had to use aerial imagery to analyze defenses and search for weaknesses, and they didn't always get it right. Fortunately I have contemporary PI *AND* post war 'ground truth' (both also sometimes flawed) to assist my annotations. Below is an enlargement of the fort entrance in 1940. The road at upper left leads past two support buildings outside the walls to a large Pakstand (anti-tank gun position) mounting two 60mm anti-tank guns and numerous machine-guns positioned to sweep the walls. The Belgians called this Block B.I. (upper left arrow). A tunnel from there led down and to the right to underground dorms, messing facilities, hospital, a power station and munitions storage 30 meters underground. All gun positions were accessed only from tunnels—note almost complete absence of paths or trails on the open ground atop the fort.

A slightly smaller Pakstand is at the wall angle to the south. White arrows inside the fort show the direction of fire from casemates each mounting three 75mm guns. Casemates are at the base of the arrows, two firing north, one south. The black arrow is what German PIs thought was one of the large-gun 5m turrets—it was a dummy.

The casemate at lower right is topped by two small armored turrets.

Enlargement shows the five meter diameter 120mm turret at upper left. I can't see one gun barrel, much less two. Intended for long-range, high angle fire against Maas River crossings north and south of the fort, those guns would be useless defending the fort itself.

At upper right the arrow indicates firing direction for another of the concrete casemate three-gun field artillery positions (Artl. Flank-Werk, 'Vise 1' to the Belgians). Those guns would sweep the interior and fire over the south wall. Arrows at lower right show a pair of three meter diameter retractable armored turrets, each with a 75mm gun. Two Pakstands along the wall were armed with 60mm anti-tank guns and machine-guns to clear the walls of attackers—very reminiscent of towers on a medieval castle. The wall ends at the steep slope down to the Albert Canal on the left.

Black arrows indicate locations of two more retractable three meter turrets mounting 75mm field pieces. If, as I suspect, the diagram above was a summation of PI work on the 1940 imagery, German PIs completely missed those gun positions. More likely they were more recent additions.

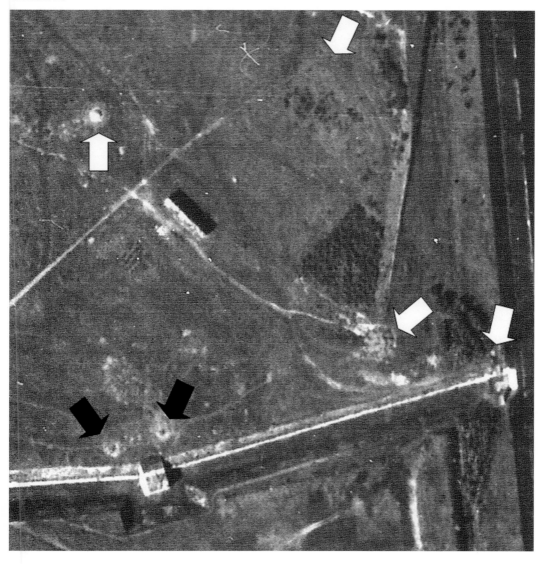

The north end of Eben Emael was equally troublesome for German PIs. Three black arrows indicate what were thought to be three of the five meter steel turrets, each with at least one 120mm howitzer. All three were decoys. Belgian camouflage discipline was excellent. Without the underground tunnels those decoys had to be planted from above and there are no tell-tale tracks left to give them away.

White arrows show more Pakstands, both positioned to control outer slopes as well as the interior of the installation with their 60mm anti-tank guns and machine-guns.

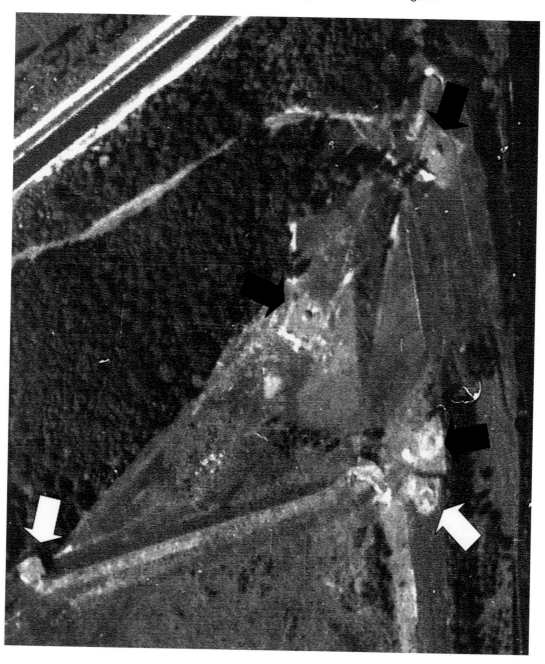

The Wehrmacht tactical solution for eliminating Eben Emael was bold and innovative. Aided by a wealth of Intelligence based upon pre-war aerial photos and ground information, every gun position, every wire line, every door and aperture were meticulously plotted. An elite force would use gliders to land on top of the fort (some sources credit Hitler with the idea). A special unit of 85 paratroopers and engineers was formed in November 1939, under Captain Koch (designated the Koch Storm Detachment). This would be the first time a glider assault was attempted and the unit trained hard in high security conditions south of Hannover, at Hidesheim, using a full-scale mock-up of Eben Emael.

Assault teams would land inside the fort in eleven DFS 230 gliders. Each team of eight men had a pre-designated objective to neutralize—gun emplacements or bridges over the Albert Canal. They would then hold the fort until on-rushing armored units could cross the river to the south and make contact. Other assault teams were to take bridges near Maastricht at Vedwezelt, Vroenhoven and Kannes, the latter just a mile NNW of Eben Emael. Tanks would start rolling west about the same time the gliders were to touch down.

It was prototypical Blitzkrieg; a well-planned and well executed surgical strike.

The DFS 230 was a new weapon but not unknown to western attachés. Towed by Ju 52 transports, eleven gliders were in the air at 0430 on 10 May 1940. The gliders released well east of the fort so aircraft motors wouldn't alert defenders. One glider was shot down and another released too early and went down in Germany, but the reduced assault force was more than enough to complete the mission. Despite some bad landings, 78 soldiers of 7th Flieger Division (elite airborne infantry) went to work immediately. With no ground combat training and no prospect of relief, Belgian garrison artillery men hadn't a clue what to do with Germans overhead dropping explosive charges down their air shafts and planting shaped charges on their armored cupolas. The first use of Top Secret shaped charges in combat was so close-hold the damage to casemates was concreted over before German authorities would allow neutral observers into the fort. A flame thrower was also used against at least one of the machine-gun positions.

The Belgian garrison surrendered at 1230 hours.

The RAF flew coverage of Eben Emael shortly after German occupation of the fort.

Note vehicle tracks breaking through the southern wall and swarming the two casemates facing to fire north (toward German Maas River crossings). This success presaged what could happen to the Maginot Line and sent the message that static defenses were not invulnerable. War of mobility had replaced trenches and forts.

The RAF photographed the fort again (shortly after the first cover, based upon more track activity inside the fort) and British Intelligence produced the graphic below. RAF PIs thought they saw two different types of gliders but it was probably light playing tricks (halation) on wings seen from different angles (it was early in the war and British PI skills were still developing). We know all the gliders were DFS 230s. Glider 2 is the more correct. Note this photo is presented upside down from the way we have been looking at the target.

FORT EBEN MAEL on the Albert Canal showing
gliders which landed in it.

GLIDER 2   GLIDER 1

56

I've annotated the base RAF imagery to show the positions of gliders (compare with previous graphic). Three gliders got pretty broken-up landing. The glider that lost its tow-cable and went down in Germany got back in the air and arrived after the fort had fallen accounting for my ten annotations.

Assault troops crossed the canal to link up with *Fallschirmjäger* in the fort. Garrison units are always weaker and less capable than troops trained to work in infantry combat and maneuver. Troops locked in fixed positions are frequently unhinged by the unexpected or the hopeless (a notable exception was Corregidor in Manila Bay two years later). One by one Eben Emael's gun positions were put out of action. Shortly after dawn the fort was neutralized. By late afternoon Allied hope of holding the Maas-Albert Canal Line was gone. The German cost was six killed and twelve wounded (some in landing).

Two miles north, bridges at Maastricht were blown by defenders but one was quickly bridged by combat engineers and German ground forces surged ahead. Seventeen days later the British Expeditionary Force began evacuation from Dunkirk. One day after that Belgium surrendered.

The assault on Fort Eben Emael is the father of all subsequent airborne operations.

The caption on this German photo says Major Witzig (in the Luftwaffe 'crusher cap') and the Captain next to him, were instrumental in taking Fort Eben Emael. 'Cooperation between Stukas, airborne and ground troops did the work in short order.'

The Major's Army Parachute Badge is peeking out from under his binocular case. Both officers wear the Iron Cross 1st Class on their breast pocket and Witzig has an Iron Cross 2nd Class at his throat. Both officers are wearing paratroop smocks and the Captain (possibly Walter Koch) has a helmet especially designed for airborne use.

The German assault on Fort Eben Emael was a small scope, extremely high risk operation with a small but highly significant pay-off. It was magnificently researched and planned, the training was near perfect. Operational execution was excellent, rapidly compensating for setbacks like loss of men caused by bad landings.

Meanwhile, in Berlin, US military attachés were collecting material related to the Eben Emael coup. This 3 August 1940 report, probably taken from a German magazine, is the citation and translation of a Knight's Cross award (highest Iron Cross Order) to another of the Eben Emael attackers. This officer and his men breached the main entrance from the outside. His award came a week after those given to men who landed inside the fort.

Obstlt. Mikosch

DNB Führerhauptquartier, 21. Mai 1940

Der Führer und Oberste Befehlshaber der Wehrmacht überreichte heute im Führerhauptquartier dem Kommandeur eines Pionier-Bataillons, Oberstleutnant Mikosch, und dem Oberfeldwebel im gleichen Bataillon Portsteffen das Ritterkreuz zum Eisernen Kreuz.

Oberstleutnant Mikosch hat unerschrocken und kühn sein Bataillon durch befestigte und zäh verteidigte Stellungen gegen das Fort Eben Emael zum Entsatz der tapferen Eroberer geführt. Dieser Tat ist es zu danken, daß das Fort endgültig gehalten werden konnte.

Fuehrer Headquarters,
May 21, 1940.

The Fuehrer and Supreme Commander of the Armed Forces in the Fuehrer Headquarters today bestowed upon the commander of a pioneer battalion, Lt. Col. Mikosch, and Oberfeldwebel Portsteffen of the same battalion, the Knights Cross to the Iron Cross.

Lt. Col. Mikosch bravely and daringly lead his battalion through fortified and strongly defended positions against Fort Eben Emael to assist the brave conquerors. It is thanks to this deed that the fort was finally held.

From : M.A., Berlin.   Report No. 17,

60

Chapter III

AN OP TOO MANY

During the Invasion of Greece in April 1941 German DFS 230s and paratroops were used in an attempt to capture Corinth Canal crossings, trapping retreating British troops. Next, airborne forces were assigned to eliminate Crete as an air and naval threat on the northern flank of German operations in North Africa. RAF bombers flying from Crete could range the eastern Mediterranean, reach Greece, Libya and southern Italy, and threaten oil fields in Ploesti, Romania. Bases on Crete also helped defend Egypt from air and sea attack.

Taking an island by airborne assault now seems like overreaching, but in the spring of 1941 the German Army was filled with hubris. To date they had only been inconvenienced or slowed, but not stopped.

CRETE

RAF Photoreconnaissance found thirty-two Ju 52s at Athens Kalamaki Airdrome on 12 May 1941. At least 31 single-engine aircraft are also present, most likely Ju 87s or fighters (to British Intelligence G.A.F. meant German Air Force). British Intelligence correctly concluded this build-up was for an invasion of Crete (which happened eight days later). The contemporary caption on this image was obviously added after the event.

ATHENS/KALAMAKI AERODROME. This photograph was taken on 12th. May, 1941, two weeks occupied by the G.A.F.
Note transport aircraft lined up for the attack on Crete.

The combined air assault on Crete would use 15,000 paratroops, 750 glider landed infantry and 5,000 regular infantry landed by shuttles of Luftwaffe transports.

Enlargement shows several generations of copying the RAF PI Report left image quality too poor to do much interpretation work. Relative aircraft size and wing shape are the only guide, starting with the largest—Ju 52s—and making an assumption about the Bf 109s (five possibles behind the transports at far left).

German paratroops suiting up in Greece for the Crete jump. Note knee pads. The thigh-length smocks were copied by British paratroopers.

Fallschirmjäger boarding a Ju 52. The small door meant troopers commonly jumped with only machine-pistols and knives. Longer, heavier weapons were dropped in color-coded canisters to be retrieved upon landing. They all wear knee pads I don't see reserve chutes but most have what looks like a static line. The photo was labeled 'Kreta'.

Invasion of Crete, Operation Mercury, was the first division-size airborne op of the war. The most important objective was Maleme Airdrome in northwestern Crete, 140 miles south of Athens. Other objectives were Suda Bay/Canea (10 miles east of Maleme), Rethymnon (10 miles farther east) and Heraklion (another 30 miles east). All objectives were on the north coast and all were attacked by at least several battalions. Landings were not mutually supporting and objectives were too many and too ambitious, but planners had no choice: the assault had to be pulled-off from the air. With no German controlled surface route to reinforce/relieve the airborne force, the assault was a gamble. The third major use of Germany's paratroop/airlift formula turned out to be 'An Island Too Far'.

The overall concept depended on jumpers taking control of Maleme on the northwest coast, permitting a large rapid infusion of infantry via Ju 52 airlift (like in Norway). A full regiment of 7th Flieger Division was assigned that task. If Maleme could not be quickly taken by storm, subsequent jumps and glider landings of reinforcements would be very expensive. That's what happened.

Crete had to be over quickly to free up transport, fighters and bombers for the scheduled Invasion of the Soviet Union, just 40 days away. On 20 May 1941 the largest combination of parachute assault and air landing to date began and met with unexpectedly heavy resistance by British, Australian, New Zealand and Greek troops.

After events in Norway and Holland, defenders guessed the objectives. Intelligence from Greece eliminated surprise. Resistance was stiff. Parachutists were shot descending and mortars destroyed gliders on landing, sometime, before their loads could get out.

New Zealand battalions defending Maleme were eventually pushed off high ground dominating the field and Maleme fell on D+2. The subsequent flood of airlift and gliderborne reinforcements doomed Crete.

Many gliders were shot down, crashed or were scattered but transport aircraft also took a beating as they brought reinforcements.

These sequential RAF photos, from 26 May 1941 (five days after the invasion), show at least 76 Ju 52s on Maleme.

Some are likely shuttling to Greece but others aren't going anywhere. Fourteen of the transports have run into each other and at least seven other planes look burned (possibly destroyed by ground fire early in the invasion). There also appear to be at least five DFS 230 gliders in the tangle of aircraft.

Enlargement of the 26 May imagery shows many haphazardly or mal-positioned planes, indicating accidents, equipment malfunctions and exhausted crews.

Athens/Kalamaki was about 1.5 hours Ju 52 flying time away, so multiple trips to Crete were possible. Airfields on Crete were to be taken by parachute infantry and immediately reinforced by glider infantry and airlifted troops. But resistance wasn't suppressed and slow-moving transports were savaged by AAA and automatic weapons fire, resulting in aircraft damage that limited a second and third lift.

Even so, 'Iron Annie' brought 35,000 troops, including the entire 5th Mountain Division, to Crete over the next few days, significantly outnumbering British, Commonwealth and Greek defenders.

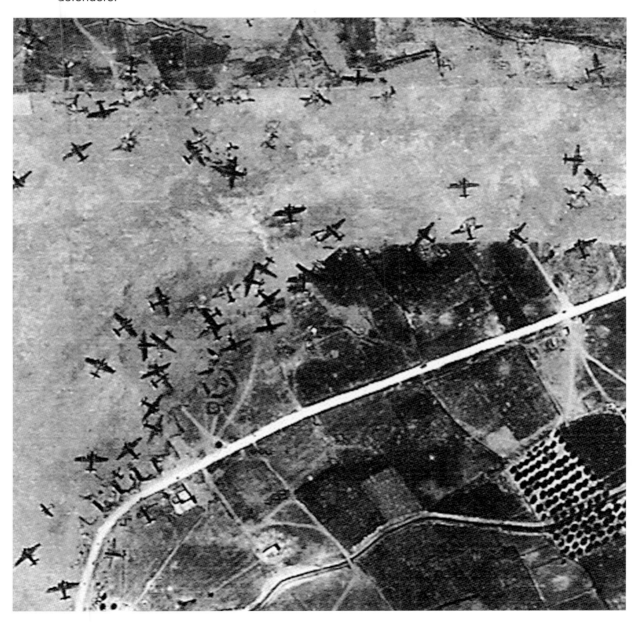

Other enlargements show Ju 52s stranded during the invasion—two in the water just off shore (left) and three on the beach (lower photo).

With Maleme still contested, on 21 May some transports landed on the beach to bring in needed weapons and reinforcements.

Taken by a British source on 10 May, different colored chutes indicate different loads—paratrooper, medicine, weapons, ammunition, food, etc.

This iconic image from the same source shows a Ju 52 going down, the pilot holding fast to his low AGL drop-run, allowing the jumpers to exit. The largest airlift/parachute landing to date was met with unexpectedly intense ground fire. This photo may be of the Battalion-size attack on Chania/Suda Bay.

Taken by a defender, probably at Suda Bay. Paratroops are still exiting the burning Ju 52. The four planes in sight are dropping 2/3 of a Rifle Company.

DZs were often ideal but the 'penny packet' landings resulting from Ju 52 inadequacy resulted in dispersed forces. Where equally dispersed defenders were nearby, jumpers suffered heavy casualties. This photo doesn't show any combat urgency.

This German open-source photo forwarded by a US military attaché in Berlin shows three Ju 52s overhead and 16 on the ground. Two Bf 110s are in the foreground beside supplies (mainly fuel drums) that have been unloaded or are about to be loaded. Location is unspecified but the leisurely stance of ground personnel (none of them under arms) and aircraft generally aligned in the same direction suggests the photo is in Greece preparing aircraft to depart for Crete.

The dust cloud almost obscuring a Ju 52 at photo center is probably from the aircraft revving-up its engines while turning. This could also be Maleme Airdrome on Crete, but I would expect to see people looking in that direction and ducking if that was an explosion from incoming. I always did. And why would those fighter planes be on the ground in Crete?

Crete was the last major German airborne assault. All three air-transport means of inserting troops in a battle are essentially offensive and the Germans were primarily on the defensive from 1943. After Crete, *Fallschirmjäger* fought as elite infantry. After mid-1944, *Fallschirmjäger* were no longer trained for jump qualification.

In January 1942 the US was a belligerent with Embassies in occupied Europe shuttered. Occurrence of foreign-source negatives on airborne activities began to dry up in the intelligence files I screened for retention 40 years later.

A DFS 230 couldn't carry artillery and Gothas weren't in use in Greece/Crete until after the invasion (and then only as transports for material, not as assault vehicles).

One of the surprises for defenders was parachute introduction of light artillery, something the cobbled-together British forces were short of. This looks like PaK 35, 37mm anti-tank gun descending under five chutes. Reportedly most of the guns dropped like this didn't survive landing, but the ones that did gave German troops a distinct advantage.

Some Ju 52s could load light artillery but not guns this large and not with the wheels on, much less parachute them from a cargo door right over the wing. It is not clear to me how heavier guns were actually airlifted. Some sources say the gun and chutes were strapped under a Ju 52 for release over the objective. The short flight from Athens could make that a possibility.

The German Airborne Invasion of Crete stands alone strategically and tactically. Unlike Norway and the Low Countries, Crete wasn't taken by surprise. The island was too large for the assigned force to easily dominate. With no clear superiority on the surrounding seas, there was little possibility of surface reinforcement (a German/Italian convoy of troops was turned back on D+1 with loss of 800 men). Defenders were equally trapped on Crete and could be expected to fight furiously. Some *Fallschirmjäger* units lost 2/3 strength in the first hour. Airfields are large objectives to take and control but they were essential to German reinforcement, so pressure was kept on Maleme.

Proximity to support bases in Greece allowed a second airlift of paratroops and gliders with heavy infantry the first afternoon. During that lift additional objectives were attacked along the north coast of Crete, apparently trying to recover the advantage of surprise. Four new battalion-size attacks spread defenses but also denied mutual support of German units in contact.

On D+7 the island was deemed lost and evacuation of defenders to Egypt began the next day. Surrender came on D+12.

The Germans lost nearly 7,000 out of 17,750 troops committed, and 370 aircraft destroyed or damaged. British and Commonwealth forces lost 17,733 men wounded, killed, or captured,

ELSEWHERE

Meanwhile, the British and Americans had noted German success with airborne operations and were busily creating their own airborne units. The British used paratroops first for raids harassing the German West Wall. Their first para-drop Commando Raid was in February 1941 to destroy a viaduct in Italy. Another such raid was on Bruneval, France in February 1942 with 100 men of 1st Parachute Battalion jumping into occupied France to capture key components of a German Search Radar. It would be many months before Allied airborne forces would be deployed in actual battalion-size or larger and engage in something other than a hit-and-run attack.

A British airborne assault on 19 November 1942 attempted to destroy the Rjukan, Norway power plant (to stop production of Heavy Water going to Germany). Operation Freshman failed when one of the tugs and both gliders employed crashed short of the target. Forty-one men were lost. Those not killed in the crash were executed by the Gestapo.

British 1st Airborne Division deployed to the Med and began small-sized operations, feeling their way.

JAPAN

On the far side of the planet, Japanese paratroops were taking Netherlands East Indies. These are Japanese Special Naval Landing Force (Marines). There were three such regiments (each actually battalion size).

The aircraft used were Nakajima Ki-34 eight passenger transports (Allied code name 'Thora') so each rank of men in this photo is a 'stick', a plane-load.

In early 1942 Japanese paratroops made jumps into Sumatra and the Celebes, taking oilfields and outflanking Singapore. They took their objectives but suffered heavy losses that pretty much ended the Japanese Navy foray into airborne operations.

This February 1942 scattered Japanese landing is on Timor, the east end of the Indonesian chain.

Japanese Army paratroops (Teishin Shudan, aka Raiding Group) boarding a Mitsubishi Ki-57 (Allied name 'Topsy'), a 15 passenger twin-engine transport. No weapons, so probably a practice jump. The Army had a brigade of paratroops and two regiments of Glider Infantry.

Japanese paratroops wore cloth-covered steel helmets and were the only ones who actually 'hit the silk'. Everyone else mostly used nylon chutes.

Palembang on the eastern end of Sumatra, February 1942. Losses in this series of assaults pretty much ended Japan's airborne operations.

I am always suspicious of 'combat' photos with a soldier coming toward the camera.

On 6 December 1944, the Japanese Army sent 750 men to destroy US planes on airfields in the Philippines. Many of their Ki-57s were shot down well short of the objectives. Some American aircraft were damaged on the ground before the attacking force was destroyed. The rest of Teishin Shudan fought the remainder of the war as regular infantry.

Japanese Navy/Marine Parachute Badge

Japanese Army
Parachute Badge.

SOVIET UNION

An early innovator and practitioner of parachute and glider operations, the Soviets never had the numbers of aircraft or the right planes to make their concepts work effectively. Stalin had 55,000 paratroops under his command when the Germans invaded but the Germans controlled the air, so he expended paratroops as infantry. He replaced the five corps (actually divisions in size) destroyed in 1941 and those too were decimated fighting as leg infantry.

An actual major airborne drop near Vyazma on 27 January 1942, 100 miles west of Moscow, went poorly and losses were high. Six drops over several days resulted in a widely scattered force on the ground that was easily decimated. Only 4,000 of the 14,000 men dropped survived, some melting into the countryside to fight as partisans. Scant information makes it hard to assess the Vyazma drop but it sounds like airborne forces were inserted in a defensive action—not what airborne infantry does best. Ground fire, or subsequent combat, taking such a toll, they must have jumped into a hornet's nest. It was just another example of the way Stalin ruthlessly expended troops to hold an untenable line rather than surrender ground for time.

A final Soviet attempt to use large unit airborne techniques occurred on 23 September 1943 near Pereyaslav, 50 miles southeast of Kiev, Ukraine.

Soviet ground forces were crossing the Dnieper on a 300 km long mass advance. The airborne operation targeted a large bend south of Kiev that formed a salient facing east. A stronghold for partisans since 1942, ground forces made good progress in the bend until 19th Panzer Division and two infantry divisions moved in opposition. It was decided to reinforce the Soviet ground action and three brigades (2000 men) were chosen to drop into the west side of the Dnieper loop. One-hundred eighty Troop carriers (mostly ancient TB-3s) and 35 gliders were used but the drops were widely scattered. Some aircraft went to 1,800' AGL to avoid flak, making a long vulnerable drop for their jumpers. Some drops were short, landing in Soviet lines on the east bank; other troops went into the river and drowned. Roughly half of the parachutists were killed landing or captured within minutes.

Paratroops preparing to board a TB-3. Did Soviet paratroops jump without helmets?

The Pereyaslav landings included parachute qualified nurses, the only females in a combat jump I know of during the Second World War.

In theory the drop was similar to Allied drops on D-Day—in practice, not so much.

Put together in haste, poor planning and preparation, not enough equipment, not enough modern troop carrier planes, poor intelligence and the worst execution of an airborne operation in the Second World War doomed the effort. Luftwaffe control of the air dictated night jumps/drops and Soviet airborne troops never formed up as a cohesive force on the west bank of the river. Many of the troops didn't know what their mission was and some didn't even know they were on a combat jump. Planned for three lifts, aircraft losses, confusion at bases and landing locations, and lack of fuel made the drop a disaster. Some troop carriers returned to base with their loads.

Below, a TB-3 with props spinning loading paratroops. I count thirteen jumpers in line, none wearing helmets and none appear to have weapons.

Above left, people to the left of the truck under the wing may be servicing the TB-3. The second group (nearer the tail) appear to be hauling/moving something—possibly more of the servicing. Under the highest magnification the image can stand, the second group look like mostly women (or men in long coats). The smaller group (beyond the tail) show banding suggesting they are wearing chutes.

What can be seen of the aircraft on the right says Sukhoi Su-2 light bombers, making this image after 1937. I found the negative in with others on Operation Barbarossa suggesting summer or fall of 1941.

Reflecting on the high cost of training, high operational losses and meager results, like Hitler after Crete, Stalin opted to use his airborne troops as infantry for the rest of the war. In 1944 the remaining Soviet airborne units were redesignated Guards Rifle Divisions, ending airborne operations by one of its pioneers.

OTHERS

Italy created, attritted and recreated parachute battalions, even divisions several times during the war, but they always fought as regular infantry.

Soviet Parachute Badge

French agents parachuted into occupied France to organize resistance against German occupation and Free French forces also mustered about 900 paratroops who fought as infantry with the British Special Air Service and in Normandy. They made no unit combat jumps.

Chapter IV

MEDITERRANEAN

Following Crete, German airborne forces had no place to go in the air. There was no German naval presence in the Med sufficient to permit an airborne assault holding non-contiguous ground farther south until relieved by land forces. Another paratroop/airlift operation like Crete was out of the question. The Libyan Desert held no opportunities. The Eastern Front offered no suitable objectives for airborne ops, and elite airborne infantry was needed on the ground to support the armored push to the east.

However, increasing Allied air and naval strength in the Med began interdicting surface supply routes to North Africa, threating to cut off the Afrikakorps. German emphasis shifted to using airlift assets for resupply. Flying from bases in Sicily, Luftwaffe transport planes attempted shuttle runs to Tunisia for resupply and reinforcement of German troops in North Africa.

AIRLIFT FAILURE

The old workhorse was called upon again, but using Ju 52s required large numbers of aircraft to ferry even moderate tonnage and the same transports were also badly needed in the Soviet Union.

Missions to North Africa from Italy could take up to three hours for the 120 to 150 miles one way, and some routes were dangerously close to the Allied hornet's nest of Malta. The tri-motor gave up more than 100 mph to intercepting aircraft and payload capacity was just over 1000 lbs., barely worth the risk of an aircraft and crew. A relatively small cargo door was also a serious limitation for the North Africa Airlift resupply program but the Luftwaffe did what it had to do.

These 10 April 1943 photos (we didn't do day/month/year then) show ten Ju 52s being intercepted by a flight of American B-25s acting as fighters (the uncropped photo shows eight B-25s). With Axis military in Libya holding on by its fingernails, desperate times called for desperate measures. Transports flying just above the water hoped to slip under Allied radar detection to reach Tunisia with critical supplies. I can find no record of this intercept so I don't know the results, but it doesn't seem to be the accidental meeting of a much faster bomber force with lumbering enemy transports.

Titling says this is 310th Bomb Group, 380th Bomb Squadron.

Got at least one.

Below, Castelvetrano, near Trapani on the western tip of Sicily, start of a 120 mile hop to Tunis. This enlargement shows four of the huge Me 323 six-engine glider-conversion transports on the ground. There were five on the field. There's that skewed tail again.

Luftwaffe transport aircraft were no longer being used for airlanding assault infantry—they were now dedicated to logistics missions, resupplying forces in combat and bringing in reinforcements.

Castelvetrano was one of the major Luftwaffe airlift bases for North Africa support. This 10 May 1943 photo shows at least 15 Ju 52s and four of the huge Me 323 six-engine transports on the field. More than fifty Ju 88s and single-engine fighters were around the field in sprawling dispersed revetments that reached up to a half mile from the landing ground (well beyond the scope of this photo).

The Afrika Korps surrendered in North Africa three days after this photo.

Allied bombing was increasingly effective in thwarting the Luftwaffe air-transport resupply program. Despite surrender in North Africa, Castelvetrano remained active. In this 28 June 1943 imagery there are no longer any Me 323s on the field and many of the revetments are empty.

Trapani-Milo Airdrome, also on the west end of Sicily, was a hotbed of Luftwaffe airborne supply missions and sweeps attacking Allied convoys heading for Malta or Alexandria. This April 1943 USAAF coverage shows one Me 323, six Ju 52, four Ju 88s, nine single-engine and eleven U/I twin-engined aircraft.

Enlargement gives a better look at the huge Me 323s. The wing striping is curious. Surely it can't be for recognition. What fighter pilot of either side would have a problem identifying that monster?

Also interesting is the middle Ju 52 in the three near photo center. It looks like it's sitting on a circle. Actually that is a powerful circular magnetic coil mounted under the plane used to detonate magnetic mines on low passes over the sea. There were two of them on this field.

A jumble of disabled aircraft and parts near the hangar (bottom) is testimony that flight from here wasn't a 'picnic.'

Earlier RAF coverage of Trapani-Milo Airdrome 140 miles northwest of Tunis shows the field loaded with Ju 52s, the aircraft most active in getting critical material to Afrika Korps.

A later RAF photo showing bombs exploding, documents the best way to interrupt an airlift. Continuing bombing like this treatment contributed to starving the Afrika Korps of fuel, rations, ammunition, replacement troops and equipment.

I ran across a curious pair of undated and unlocated small-scale RAF negs showing German glider activity. This is clearly in North Africa, almost certainly the Libyan Desert.

There are more than 20 aircraft in revetments at top and bottom, most of them single-engined. The Accession Numbers that located these negatives in US Intelligence Files (lower right) are early, so 1943 is likely. The activity caught my eye as unusual but I have no information on this pair.

Even more vexing, this could be a training flight, but why train gliders in North Africa? Where could the small glider go? What could it do? Was it used as a taxi to take people to Crete, Greece or between Tunis and points east? Or, could it be training for a commando mission?

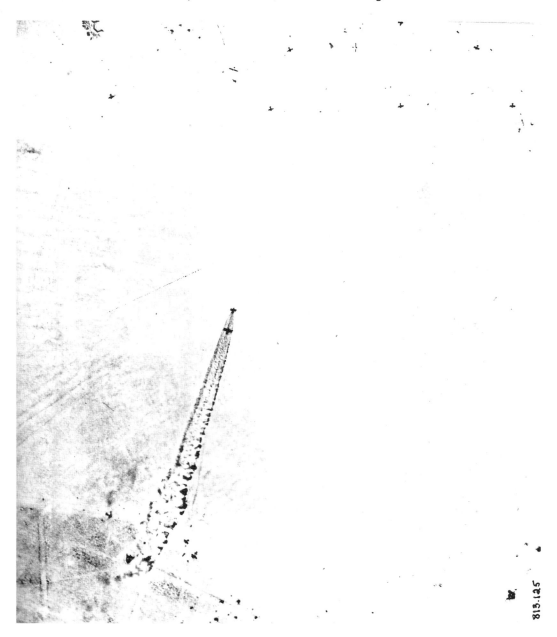

Want to do a little PI? Assume the glider is a DFS 230 (the only choice available in 1943). That's a 72 foot wing span. For comparison, a Ju 87 wingspan is 45 feet. We're seeing both the object and its shadow. Shadow is good for shape and what I see of the tow-plane wing says 'Stuka'. Measurements are best made on the object itself.

So, do you agree with my interpretation based upon wing shape and span ratios?

Below, the tow-plane is just off the photo and shadow shows the glider is about 30 feet above the ground.

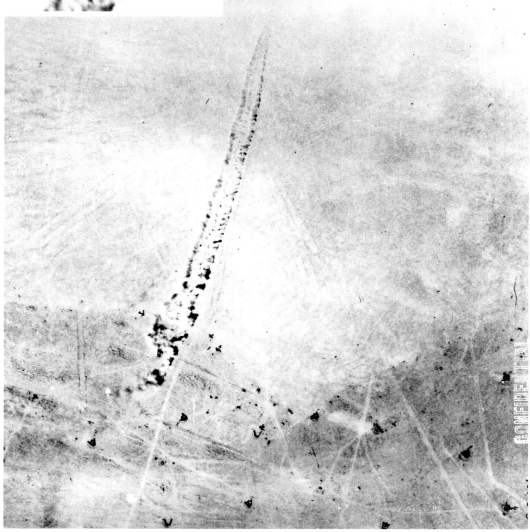

WANING AND WAXING

Following the Pyrrhic victory on Crete, German interest in paratroop and glider landing operations faded even as Allied interest and capability surged.

Men of 509th PIR made the first US combat jump. Scheduled airborne landings in Operation Torch (Invasion of North Africa—Nov 42) failed when aircraft couldn't locate DZs and landed on a dry lake bed. The highly-motivated paratroops of the 509th, disappointed by their first outing, marched off to find their objectives—establishing a tradition that continued through the war. It became SOP that no matter where they were put down, paratroopers immediately moved toward their targets.

ALL THE WAY

509th PIR

A few small, scattered 'Commando-Style' airborne operations were traded across the Mediterranean, but nothing major until the Invasion of Sicily on 9 July 1943.

Operation Husky (Invasion of Sicily, Jul 43) was the largest on-shore assault to date (actually larger than Overlord a year later). Both jumps and airlanding were used—and that part of the invasion was almost as disastrous as Crete. The US Army contributed the 505th Parachute Infantry Regiment; the UK used their 21st Independent Parachute Company plus the 1st Airlanding Brigade. Those units made contributions but were 'side shows' to troops landing over the beaches. The 505th made the first Allied Regimental-sized combat jump of the war.

505th PIR

Troopers of 82nd AD helping each other suit-up for the Husky jump. Some helmets have camouflage webbing and each man seems to have shovel. Pockets are stuffed with essentials like food, ammo and medical supplies. Reserve chutes are on the ground and will be hooked on just before boarding the C-47. Weapons must be nearby.

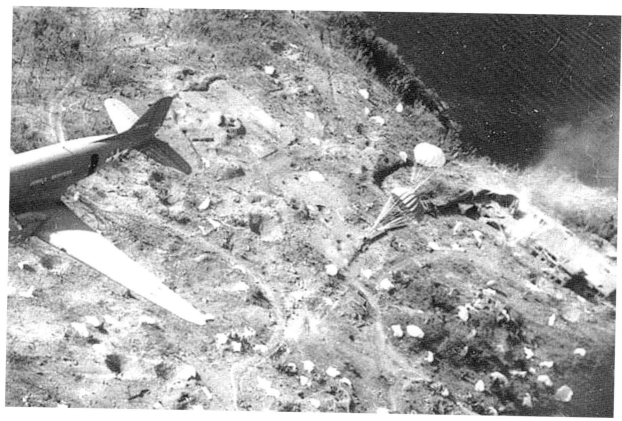

Early Allied use of airborne forces proved planners didn't understand how to best exploit the advantages of the weapon. It's hard to understand how someone thought it was a good idea to drop men right on the coast, instead of open, undefended, ground farther inland. Rough ground, bomb craters and enemy trenches/defense revetments made for less than ideal DZ but none of the airborne ops in Sicily were pretty.

Lessons learned were that parachute infantry can land almost anywhere, but gliders had trouble on the heavily broken terrain and narrow valleys. Tow-planes faced high winds and couldn't compensate, so the landings were badly scattered. Twelve out of 147 gliders were on target and 69 went down in the water off-shore. In the drop at Gela on the southeast coast, just 400 of the 1600 paratroops sent out actually reached the target. Transport crews also learned not to fly routes anywhere near the navy during night operations. Twenty-three C-47s were shot down by friendly fire.

Operation Avalanche (Invasion of Italy, Sep 43) had a rare defensive use of airborne ops. On 13 and 14 September 1943 the 82nd AD's 504th and 505th PIRs were dropped inside Allied lines to reinforce the beachhead at Salerno, Italy. Lt. General Mark Clark, Fifth Army Commander, said the paratroops' timely arrival and aggressive combat were 'responsible for saving the Salerno beachhead'.

DUELING DROPS

The Germans and British traded airborne initiatives six miles south of Catania on the east coast of Sicily. A 400' steel girder bridge over the Simeto River was the only crossing and the key to Catania, just to the north. The Germans wanted it to keep control of the city and port. The British wanted the bridge as a route to Catania and Messina and to prevent German evacuation to the Italian mainland. So both planned battalion-sized parachute jumps to take the Primosole Bridge.

On 13–14 July 1943 British 1st Parachute Brigade was to jump north of the bridge and 2nd Brigade to the south, gliders would come in next.

The Operation Fustan assault was a 'cock up' from the start. Again Allied tow-planes got too close to trigger-happy Allied sailors and some were shot down. Others scattered. Then the Germans opened up and destroyed another 37. Only 39 C-47s got their jumpers anywhere near the target, and those drops were scattered. Four gliders made it in unscathed and close to their objectives.

Worse yet, 3rd Parachute Regiment of 1st *Fallschirmjäger* jumped to the bridge first, behind where some British units were to land. 1st Para Bde took the bridge, then lost it and suffered many casualties and PoWs. The bridge changed hands several times before going firmly into British hands on 15 July when tanks arrived from the south. By that time the Germans had established a solid defense line north of the bridge and Catania didn't fall until 5 August.

Both landings were brigade-sized and demonstrated the tenacious, highly focused spirit that came to characterize airborne infantry on both sides. The Primosole Bridge assaults were pretty much a failure for the British; less so for the Germans, who gained the time they needed to pull back and regroup for evacuation to mainland Italy.[8]

A REPRIEVE

Following Husky many American generals who had been enthusiastic about airborne assault possibilities began to have doubts. General Eisenhower questioned whether large airborne units could be controlled (directed) in combat. This was in part because it was difficult to get them on the ground in the right place and without excessive losses. Given the communications of the day, it was also difficult to know where the airborne units were, their strength and condition until after they linked to ground forces.

In December 1943 a test maneuver was set up to have the untried 17th Airborne Division land paratroops and glider infantry to capture Knollwood Army Auxiliary Airfield. A defending force was of equal size. The 17th had one PIR and two glider infantry regiments so 200 C-47s carried jumpers and two other transport groups towed 234 Waco gliders to Knollwood. The night operation on 7 December was a success with 85 percent of the 4,800 men landing on target about 15 miles WNW of Fort Bragg, North Carolina.

All objectives taken by dawn.

Adherents were encouraged by Knollwood but two important points were apparently glossed over. There was no ground fire opposing the landings to shoot down aircraft and gliders or 'spook' troop carrier pilots causing the landings to scatter. Further, the eleven different targets to assault were geographically close and readily identifiable from the air at night.

Following Knollwood, division-sized airborne operations were again contemplated by planners—just in time as it turned out.

---

8. Because the Germans jumped first to take the bridge I don't consider that a defensive use of airborne infantry.

Chapter V

PACIFIC INITIATIVES

After an initial brute force strategy in New Guinea pushing troops forward at all costs in appalling conditions, trading lives for land, General Douglas MacArthur halted Japanese advances in the Southwestern Pacific—and learned a lesson. From then on he opted for more sophisticated campaigns whenever possible, gradually earning a justifiable reputation for not wasting his troops. He took far more land with fewer losses than any of the generals in Europe, not the least because of clever, sometimes brilliant, offenses that caught his less mobile, less imaginative (and usually less well equipped) enemies flat-footed. Even when such slashing leaps might be expected, the enemy could never be sure when and where the hammer would fall.

MacArthur had followed with great interest the airborne capability being developed by the American and British Armies, and their stumbling initial operations. In December 1942 he had been given 503rd PIR and wanted to try it out, but its debut had to be a success.

Operation Postern was the result, a pincers advance designed to outflank Japanese forces around the stronghold of Lae, New Guinea, neutralizing them or forcing them to withdraw. Australia's 9th Infantry Division came ashore east of Lae and a day later the US 503rd Parachute Infantry Regiment (PIR) was to land and create a forward base on the north side of the Owen Stanley Range, cutting off an enemy retreat. Eight crews of Australian field artillerymen were anointed as paratroops and dropped with their cut-down 25-pounder guns to provide artillery support. After paratroops took control of the area, the Australian 7th Infantry Division was to be airlifted in to press toward their comrades on the coast.

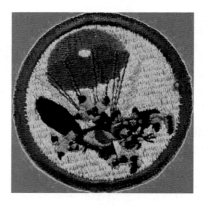

503rd PIR

The site chosen for the air-drop/airlift part of the operation was Nadzab, an abandoned airfield in the Markham Valley, some 20 miles northwest of Lae. There was plenty of space for fast, concentrated parachute landings (no gliders in the Pacific at the time).

Allied reconnaissance indicated the area was apparently not occupied by the Japanese and the old airfield could quickly be put into service for airlift of troops and supplied.

Not exactly an assault, more like an occupation.

NADZAB

The files I searched contained a complete set of original 9" x 18" Nadzab contact prints taken by a hand-held K-18 aerial camera (including an occasional fingerprint from a careless photo tech developing the film). I have included my favorites here. Because a full print exceeds the size I can scan, where the entire format is needed, I scanned a print twice, down-sized and reassembled the segments. Film titling indicates there were at least two of the big aerial cameras (provided by 8th Photo Squadron) used in two different planes. Most of the photos appear to have been shot from a circling 498th Bomb Squadron B-25—those are the ones showing a section of the right wing.

On the morning of 5 September 1943, surprise, and control of the Markham Valley (above) was swiftly achieved when B-25s appeared overhead to strafe the landing area (some of it in tall grass) and drop small fragmentation bombs to clear out any Japanese that might be hiding on the ground.

91

A closer look at some of the B-25s and dozen P-38 fighters (lower right) covering the landing. By this time many B-25s in SWPAC were retrofitted with multiple nose guns and used more for ground attack straffing than bombing.

Below, low-flying A-20s laid down smoke to mask the landing sites.

Aligning on the smoke, troop carrier C-47s came in low and tight with one flight right behind the other and aircraft staged up to avoid chutists in the air. The selected DZ couldn't have been better; open, flat, few trees.

All 6,000 men were unloaded in less than five minutes.

Enlargement from the previous photo. This series is the best imagery I've ever seen of a combat parachute drop. Sticks were out of their transports in 10 seconds. You can see the troopers swinging and landing at top and bottom and note how low the troop carrier planes were. Jumps were made from between 400 and 500 feet altitude. Paratroopers had hardly swung vertical and they were on the ground. An unopposed drop made this possible.

Each Battalion had its own DZ so assembly on the ground was very fast.

Photo technicians with hand-held aerial cameras were shooting out the windows of several circling aircraft, including the B-17 command ship. Low collection altitude, large lenses and large film size returned exceptionally good imagery of the operation. Presence of low-flying photographers indicates confidence in little or no ground opposition.

With top cover orbiting, eighty-four 54th Troop Carrier Wing C-47s brought in 1,700 men of the 503rd PIR for the Pacific's first Allied paratroop drop. Coming from eight different airfields near Port Moresby, 302 planes rendezvoused and were over the jump area on schedule. Drops began at 1022 hours local and the entire area was secured within 24 hours.

The photo above is interesting because it shows the main drop area (bottom) and another drop zone in the distance with a plane on a perpendicular course (heading away from the camera).

Another C-47 (left arrow) is just above the tree line (not dropping yet). The same distance to the right (right arrow), just above the tree line, a P-38 flying away from the camera, trolls for trouble, protecting the DZs.

Between the two arrows (above) is a C-47 flying away from the camera. Enlargement shows the first (lowest) two chutes may be a tandem drop, suggesting something particularly heavy. This may be the Australian artillery unit drop. Reinforced floor and wide double doors on some C-47s permitted para-drop of large equipment or palletized supplies.

The photo below shows the main drop with flights of four aircraft abreast streaming from lower right to center left where the chutes from the first flight are close-spaced over the open field. Note the B-17 'command ship' circling overhead (upper right).

Enlargement shows one flight over the DZ and the next getting ready to drop. Low altitude, close spacing of aircraft and fast exit from the planes made for tight groups of men landing.

The same place a few seconds later shows more of the tightly grouped chutes coming down. Aircraft overhead are P-38s making sure Japanese fighters from nearby Lae didn't interfere with the operation.

Flights of aircraft were sequencing so close they were dropping troopers while men from previous flights descending below them were still in the air. Illustrating how fast the actual drop went, I can see 18 C-47s in this photo from the far left margin to the ones silhouetted against the smoke on the right that have yet to drop.

I put two images together to show more of the area. At original photo scale this measures 36" from side-to-side.

Enlargement of the previous photo shows a seemingly dangerous situation with three low-flying B-25s heading directly into the mass of descending paratroops and on an intercept course with the transport planes. I found no record of accident or injury from converging courses like this so I guess the B-25 drivers avoided everyone else in this busy air.

In another curious event (below), chutes at photo center are from a C-47 just above the last parachute and heading on a reciprocal course to the stream of transport aircraft heading towards us. With the B-17 command ship overhead, one has to assume the different drop area (in dense trees) is either on purpose for some reason not apparent in the photo—or the troop carrier pilot is turned around and will get a real 'wire-brushing' after landing.

Enlargement of the 'wrong place, wrong direction' drop. The C-47 is at the arrow, heading away from the camera and the chutes are going down in trees where jump injuries might be expected or supply canisters harder to retrieve.

Below, a good photo of drop spacing—a little slow getting out the door by later airborne standards.

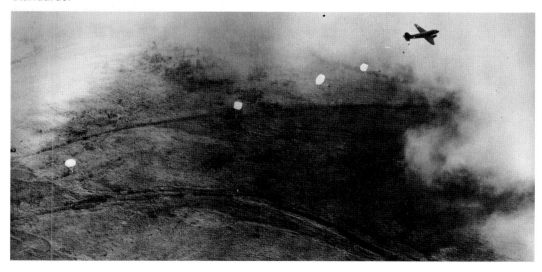

Aircraft shadows at photo bottom are from the planes at far left, giving an idea of drop altitude.

Density of chutes on the ground proves how tight the drop was—ideal but probably possible only with little or no ground or air opposition.

Operation Postern was better and closer covered by imagery than any other airborne operation until Corregidor (later in this book). As the largest and most successful US paradrop to date, Nadzab encouraged parachute advocates in Washington, DC and was studied to plan airborne operations for Overlord ten months later. One of the lessons should have been that a low daylight drop resulted in very little scattering of the men and rapid assembly on the ground as a fighting force.

Well planned, well timed and well executed, the Nadzab initiative had good weather, clear daylight and complete suppression of any potential opposition, quickly resulting in achievement of all planned objectives with remarkably light casualties (3KIA, 33 injured).[9] Linkage with ground troops coming along the shore occurred in three days. The op didn't result in trapping the Japanese Army but in a week, engineers created two parallel runways and 25th INF Bde (Aus) Field Regt. was airlifted in to the Markam Valley. Nadzab became a hub for subsequent offensive and logistic action on New Guinea's north coast, making possible taking Lae on16 September and eliminating a major Japanese base at Salamaua.

That set up conquest of the Huon Peninsula and taking of Finschhafen which further tightened the noose on the major Japanese hub at Rabaul.

Several photos show a B-17 circling the area, acting as a command ship with General MacArthur aboard. The general was famously photographed pointing past a .50 cal. waist gun with obvious delight at the apparent success. His air-chief, Major General George Kenney, wrote to USAAF chief, General H. H. Arnold that MacArthur was so excited watching the drop he was 'jumping around like a kid'.

It is unlikely the general could have intervened to change anything happening during the drop, on the ground or in the air, but MacArthur was subsequently awarded an Air Medal for personally directing the operation from the air (it was about the only medal he didn't already have, and diligent Staff Officers always ensure the boss gets decorated).

---

9. Some sources cite over 100 KIA and 241 wounded/injured.

DUMMIES

Dummy parachutists were used several times during the war to dupe ground forces as to the location, size and intent of an actual airborne op. An early use was during the German invasion of the Netherlands in 1940, magnifying confusion for the defenders. Though not part of an airborne operation, the Germans used dummy paratroops to some effect in the Ardennes during the Battle of the Bulge in 1944.

Nadzab was the first American use with dozens of decoys dropped between the Markham Valley and Lae to convince Japanese defenders that the operation was larger. Adding little, like the basic Op, the dummies were overkill to guarantee success.

Operation Titanic on 6 June 1944 saw perhaps as many as 500 British burlap and sand dummies, code named 'Ruperts,' dropped in four locations 10 miles inland along the French coast north of Rouen—60 miles east of Overlord landings. That effort drew at least one German rifle regiment away from Overlord beaches.

Dummies were also dropped near Marigny, France, some five miles west of St Lo and 15 miles south of actual US paradrops. They added to the confusion but didn't change any German troop dispositions.

There is a question as to whether the more realistic American inflatable parachutist dummies, 'Oscars,' were used in Normandy but they were certainly used near Marseille during Operation Dragoon in August 1944.

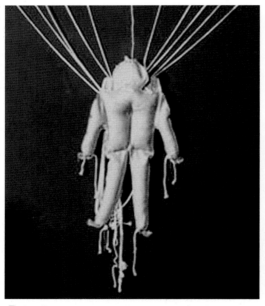

Rupert.

Oscar.

NEW GUINEA AGAIN

On 3–4 July 1944, the 503rd Parachute Infantry Regiment was in the air again to assist the invasion of Noemfoor Island, Dutch New Guinea which was already in progress. Their objective was one of three airfields on the island. First Battalion was to reinforce regular infantry facing heavy resistance. Casualties were heavy, mostly leg injuries from bad landings caused by jumping too low. The drop was planned for 300' AGL but because of pilot error came off at 150' AGL.

Chapter VI

DIVISION-SIZE ASSAULT

Nothing on the scale of D-Day's assault on a well-defended shore (Operation Overlord) had ever been attempted. Six infantry divisions would land at five locations along 40 miles of Normandy Beach. The scope of the invasion was as staggering as the obstacles to be overcome ashore. Planners knew it would be touch-and-go until sufficient force could be built-up, and they pulled out all the stops. Beachheads had to be quickly deepened to effective defensive perimeters. There would be swimming tanks, artificial harbors and a fuel pipeline under the English Channel. Direct fire from ships off invasion beaches and bombing by heavy, medium, light and fighter bombers would isolate the invasion area and impede enemy reinforcements coming up. Disrupting enemy troop movements behind the invasion beaches was a high priority, and weeks before D-Day Allied fighter and bomber aircraft began interdicting lines-of-communication as far north and east as Paris.

Operations in the Mediterranean proved what airborne units could do and strength had grown to four full Divisions: US 82nd and 101st and British 6th (British 1st Airborne was in England but not assigned to Overlord). There was never any doubt about elite American and British parachute and airlanding infantry units being in the mix. They became Operation Neptune.[10]

Of course the Germans knew an invasion was coming, they just didn't know when or where. So they steadily improved passive and active defenses all along the Atlantic coast from Norway to the Bay of Bisque, starting with what they considered the most likely beaches and air landing locations (in the Pas de Calais).

Much as the British had done in Kent in 1940, defenders seeded obstructions into large open fields where airborne troops might land. Posts called 'Rommelspargel' (Rommel asparagus) were little hindrance to paratroops but they were a real hazard for gliders,

designed to tear off wings or flip them onto their backs.[11] Some posts had Teller Mines on top.

However, surprise and swift use of a concentrated force landing near ground objectives were crucial, so static defenses like these were noted but largely disregarded in Allied assault planning.

---

10. See my book *The Normandy Invasion*, Pen & Sword 2012.
11. The American officer in the photo was part of an OSS team that documented defenses after D-Day.

Every possible airborne landing glider and parachute site was covered by Allied aerial recon in the search for suitable fields near tactical objectives. This is a broad, flat, dry area on the Vire River, near the Caen-Cherbourg rail line (seen at upper right). It is three miles south of Isigny sur Mer on 28 May 1944, (six miles SSE of Utah Beach).

Those white dots show spoil from vertical posts, 'Rommel Asparagus,' set out in rows to interrupt a glider landing. German engineers apparently deemed the east side of the Vire too marshy for a glider landing. No Allied airborne landings were planned for here.

British aerial photos of the invasion area went back to 1942, so they had plenty to study for selection of LZ/DZs. With many large open fields and relatively few passive defenses, landing locations were selected based upon proximity to mission objectives. From left to right on the Channel coast is: Sword Beach, the Caen Canal, Orne River, a small gun battery (arrow), and the site of future Merville Battery of heavy guns (lower arrow). Two key bridge objectives are just off the lower left. The main British LZ is at bottom center.

Time denied the same depth of photo recce and study over American potential LZs and DZs. All 82nd and 101st AD could do to prepare was select good objectives (mostly bridges) and hope their LZs and DZs were viable—then train hard, making sure each man knew what to expect and what his tasks were.

The need for surprise made night drops and glider landings unavoidable. Based on earlier operations, high casualties and confusion were anticipated, but weighed against taking pressure and attention off the beaches, the risk was deemed acceptable.

No one was under any illusions that surprise would result in unopposed Neptune landings, and 82nd Airborne's 505th Parachute Infantry Regiment (PIR) was the only unit jumping that had prior experience in combat (Operation Husky in July 1943). Airborne Units stepped up training in England knowing they would be the first to contact the enemy and their failure could jeopardize the entire invasion.

Moon reflection off the Orne River gave 6th AD an excellent guide for tow and glider pilot navigation at midnight. LZs/DZs were only three to six miles from the landing beaches so, unless the invasion failed, link-up should be quick—if infantry coming over the beaches didn't get stalled.

The 82nd and 101st had the same screening mission but also many point objectives: causeways, important intersections and bridges – perhaps too many; dividing their force.

British emphasis was on a few paratroops securing landing sites and removing obstacles so gliders could land the bulk of their force. Americans favored most of an airborne division's strength jumping in, followed by gliders near daylight with heavy equipment, supplies and reinforcements. So, on the east flank large, open LZs (Landing Zones) were more important than parachute DZs (Drop Zones) with the reverse on the west. Fortunately, terrain in the east was better suited for large glider landings and parachuting into boccage country in the west was better for the more numerous, scattered point targets on the west flank,

A-6M6-FRANCE-ST.MERE EGLISE-N4924 WO119-CONFIDENTIAL
1679.607

Training in England was intensive with gliders practicing flight and landing through April 1944. Shadows are well out in front of the aircraft but the spread is less on the lead ships. The C-47 at upper right is atop the shadow of the Waco CG-4 it is towing, showing this flight is descending. In a live operation the planes would be much closer together.

The scope of Neptune is evident in this aerial photo of a single UK base training glider pilots in May 1944. I count 19 C-47 tow-planes, 24 Horsa gliders in two-tone British camouflage livery, 78 Waco gliders with US markings and olive drab paint, one B-24, one U/I light plane and one possible B-25. And this is only part of one base. For some reason the serial of Waco gliders and C-47 tugs lined up for take-off is short one glider.

For size and shape comparison, this enlargement shows a C-47 troop carrier/glider tug, a Horsa glider and two American Waco gliders. You will see these shapes again and again on the following pages.

The well-known black and white Invasion recognition stripes weren't applied until the first days of June.

In the east, the left flank of Overlord, 8,000 men of 6th Airborne would land at six locations, each with a specific, limited objective (five point targets and one functional mission). This part of Neptune was Operation Tonga.

Heavy guns in the Merville Battery (three miles east of what would be Sword Beach at dawn) were to be neutralized by 1st Canadian and 9th British Parachute Battalions. Brigade-sized parachute and glider landings east and west of the Orne and Caen Canal at Benouville-Ranville would take two key bridges and control the only viable route for German attacks on Overlord's east flank. A parachute landing (3rd Brigade and 8th Battalion) would drop farther southeast to function as a trip wire for the expected German counter-attacks from the east and southeast.

The two American airborne divisions would screen the right (west) flank with 12,000 men each. They'd been assigned many point and area objectives to cover. They had to secure causeways over swampy ground, bridges and crossroads on key routes for use by friendlies advancing south from Utah Beach, or to deny them to German reinforcements.

Everyone understood that the Normandy Invasion would begin with airborne infantry going in first and night airborne ops had proven unpredictable. The drops/landings had to be spot-on and tight for the best chance of success—and none of the troop carrier pilots in Overlord had experience flying into anti-aircraft fire.

It was also understood by all involved that if the invasion failed on the beaches, all three divisions of airborne infantry would be lost.

D-DAY

Parachute assault would require C-47s to overfly the objectives, alerting defenders. Instead, just after midnight on 5/6 June, six Horsas dropped their tow-cables northeast of Caen and silently carried D Company, 2nd Oxfordshire and Buckinghamshire Light Infantry north to within feet of their objective (LZs Y and X). Eben Emael's lessons had been learned. The small assault force swiftly assembled and controlled both bridges in ten minutes—liberating the first piece of France and beginning the invasion.

Looking north, a photo of LZ X taken just after dawn shows a Horsa, and the wing of another, a few feet from the bascule bridge spanning the Caen Canal east of Benouville. The bridge counter-weight is visible at upper left, as are German trenches on the east side of the canal. The bridge was taken in minutes and the Orne River Bridge, 2000' east, shortly after. Honoring this coup, the Orne River Bridge is now named for British Horsa gliders and the Caen Canal Benouville Bridge for Pegasus, the 6th Airborne Division emblem.

Radioing control of the bridge launched the rest of the division to land two hours later. In spite of high winds scattering some drops, 6th AD made a 'text book' landing, on target at all six locations, accomplishing all assigned tasks by dawn.

When a flood of infantry began to arrive from the air, the Germans were just as unable to sort out and stop what was happening as were the Dutch and Belgians in 1940.

However, at dawn, Overlord Headquarters was almost as much in the dark.

RAF and USAAF Photo Recce aircraft lifted off for France before first light on 6 June. Extensive cloud cover would ordinarily scrub a photo mission, but not this day. It was critical to determine what was going on in France. Were the airborne landings on target and were they successful? London knew the two bridges north of Caen were the only avenue for a German flank attack on the east. Were they still being held or was the left flank in danger?

Seventeen gliders can be seen on this near dawn small-scale RAF exposure near the Ranville quarry (bottom center), between Amfreville and Ranville (Landing Zone N). The Orne River is down and to the left with the Caen Canal beyond to the west. North, and the Atlantic coast, are to the top of the photo. Most of 6th AD's 5th Parachute Brigade and 6th Airlanding Brigade were on the ground here by dawn.

Enlargement of the previous photo shows the sort of thing that makes a PI look closer. Regularly spaced white dots running in a straight line to the upper left corner suggest a newly installed phone line. Disregarding farm field boundaries says it's military—perhaps related to the Merville Battery. Other nearby smaller dots in the fields (random and slightly closer together) show locations of 'Rommelspargel' set out to disrupt glider landings.

Clearly 6th AD paratroops didn't have time to remove all the obstacles prior to arrival of the gliders and some were damaged landing.

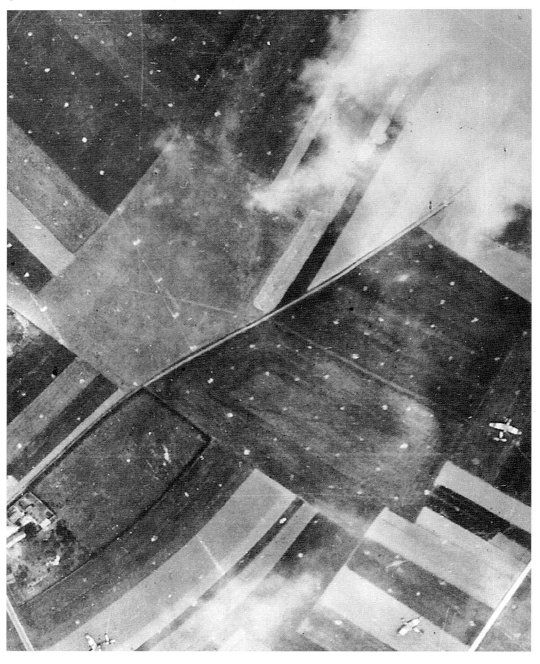

This is looking southwest at the 6th AD primary landing area (LZ N). The Orne River and Caen Canal are on the right. A little bit of Benouville shows just beyond the cloud at upper right (on the far side of the canal). The bridge objectives are directly under the cloud (a not uncommon disappointment for a PI). The dark curving shape at upper left is the port propeller of the taking aircraft, an American F-5 (P-38 photo recon version). Clustered chutes can be seen just right of the propeller tip and 40 gliders are seen on the ground—one between the river and canal (LZ Y) just north of the bridges (just beyond the cloud). Other gliders came down in fields just beyond the right of this frame (LZ W). Operation Mallard landings had 246 of 256 gliders arrive by morning—all within a mile of the bridge objectives.

Main force gliders landed around dawn, towed inland past the LZ, releasing and turning back north, using light reflecting off the water courses for navigation to hit their obviously well-selected LZ. All gliders, original assault and reinforcement, appear to have landed heading in the same direction, heading toward the coast (toward the bottom of this photo).

For orientation with modern maps, that white blob on the ground just below the cloud is the quarry north of Ranville.

Enlargement of the previous photo shows it must have been taken quite early on 6 June because on the next page is a photo showing the same area with more than a dozen additional gliders in the same fields where chutes are on the ground in this photo. An even later photo shows at least 80 gliders in this Landing Zone.

Further enlargement of the photo above shows eighteen Horsas and a possible Hamilcar (at upper left). The Hamilcar has straight wings—and is facing west (to the right) rather than north (down) like the Horsas, suggesting a different landing wave or time. Assembling these men and their equipment into a viable combat force and positioning them to meet counter-attacks would have been fast, even in the early light. Mallard was a good landing site choice and good landing execution.

Looking at the recognizable field patterns of LZ/DZ N from the other direction. There are many more gliders on the ground. This photo may be from D+1. I see three possible Hamilcars. Overlord was their first combat use.

For those who want to do a little PI and try to ID the Hamilcars, span, leading wing edge angle and method of opening are the keys to identification. (photo courtesy of Pat Curran)

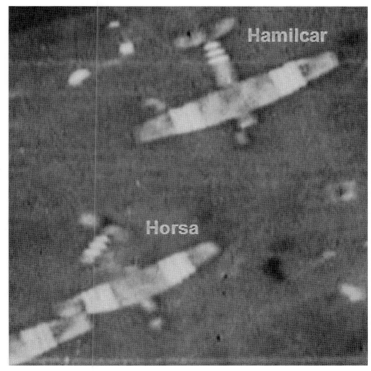

Another enlargement of USAAF-flown imagery northeast of the Ranville Quarry early on 6 June shows two examples of unremoved 'Rommelspargel' clipping the wings of gliders. In two cases the wing has been cut off at the Invasion recognition stripes, but the gliders didn't flip over. Other Horsas seem to have avoided hazards and got down without disaster.

Landing in LZ V west of Varaville following sharp fighting, 1st Canadian and 9th British Parachute Battalions neutralized the Merville Battery before Sword Beach landings began at dawn. The Battery was discovered to have four obsolete 100mm guns instead of the expected more threatening, modern 150mm guns.

Headquarters 3rd Parachute Brigade and 8th Parachute Battalion landed at DZ K, five miles southeast of LZ N to blunt German attacks from the east. The 6th AD Commanding General commendably placed himself in the most vulnerable location, then diluted his gesture by using 47 of his precious C-47 sorties to lift the Headquarters and Staff instead of troops closer to the point of the spear. The photo below is at Herouvillette, southeast of Ranville. Halfway between landing zones N and K, this may be part of the headquarters landing. There are cargo and paratroop chutes, Rommelspargel and mine fields showing.

The top of this enlargement has chutes in a passive defense field; some appear to have drop canisters still attached. The close-space white dots at bottom are a probable mine field, and German trenching at lower right indicates presence of German troops.

Canisters with heavy loads often accompanied jumps to keep from adding weight on the paratroopers. Separate canister drops were used to resupply units already on the ground. This one is 6,000 feet northwest of Sainte-Marie-du-Mont on the western flank of the Invasion.[12] Typically chutes with canisters still attached will fill with air long after the drop while jump-chutes and chutes with canisters detached will usually collapse and remain flat on the ground.

---

12. Thanks to Pat Curran for helping identify this and other locations in this section. He and his Forum members, **http://www.normandy.whitebeamimages.ie/forum/index.php,** are doing fantastic forensic analysis of D-Day Airborne landings and crash sites.

Chutes with canisters still attached and a single unattached canister at upper right indicate a recent drop.

Some canisters were dropped along with the parachute infantry but most were dropped separately to quickly resupply troops on the ground;

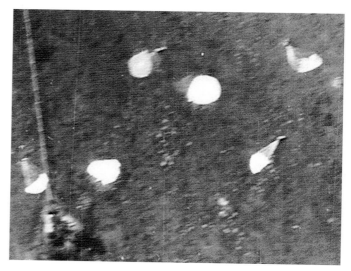

Parachute containers were used to deliver medicine, ammunition, food, even weapons. The standard was a six foot by 15" diameter CLE (Central Landing Establishment) container developed by the British. Markings on the outside identified contents to facilitate unloading in combat. The photo below (date and location unknown) shows loading a CLE with rounds for a PIAT (Projectile, Infantry, Anti-Tank).

More USAAF aerial photo reconnaissance of the 6th Airborne Division landing, this time on D+1, looking southeast. Large flat, open fields; one couldn't wish for a more perfect glider landing site. The first of these 46 Horsas came in just before dawn on 6 June. A day later the war had already moved south and east. At the right edge are bombed German defense positions and tank tracks heading inland. Caen is five miles straight ahead. This is British LZ W on the west side of the Caen Canal (which can be seen at upper left) between Benouville/LePort (arrow) and Saint-Aubin d'Arquenay (lower left). Pegasus Bridge is where the road crossing the frame and the canal intersect (just above the left side of the photo). Like LZ N, just over the Orne, landings here were made from south-to-north (toward photo bottom).

Lord Lovat's Commandos followed the canal bank path south from Sword Beach, the skirl of bagpipes famously preceding them. They linked up with 6th Airlanding Brigade at Pegasus Bridge just after 1300 hours on D-Day. Reinforced by infantry advancing from Sword Beach, British 6th Airborne Infantry held the ground east of the Orne for several more days in the face of determined German counter-attacks.

Sharp eyes will pick up three well spaced-out probable British Armored Cars heading inland from Sword Beach on the road (which no longer exists) running diagonally across the center of the frame.

Enlargement of 6th Airborne Division Landing Zone W shows landings to be tight and clean despite occurring before dawn. It is interesting that an obviously perfect glider landing area close to military positions and objectives, right beside the Orne and just two miles south of Ouistreham, wasn't filled with passive defense obstacles. The only field that is suspicious is the one at bottom center. Digging is regular and close-spaced (usually meaning mines) but not as close as other mine fields I've seen in Normandy. My gut says it's 'Spargel.'

OVERLORD'S RIGHT FLANK

The 4th Infantry Division's Utah Beach landing was added to Overlord with just six months to prepare. Twelve miles west of the other beaches, Utah was unconnected and unsupported by the rest of the invasion. A two-division American airborne component to support 4th ID was approved on 1 April 1944. The scramble began to identify objectives, good drop and landing sites. Too much photo recon concentration could tip the enemy to landing locations, so many photo missions were disguised inside the on-going hunt for V-Weapons launch sites which the Germans were used to. A few good and several passable drop locations emerged. Terrain was boccage, ancient small pastures framed by almost impenetrable stone and hedge borders. Not much problem for jumpers but hell for gliders.

American airborne commanders wanted support artillery brought in by glider in the first wave but night landing exercises in mid-April resulted in so many crashes that gliders were slated for daylight operations.

Because Utah was added so late in Overlord planning, the two US airborne divisions would land directly inland from the beach rather than farther west as a screen. Untested 101st AD was to take and hold dry causeways through what were thought to be impassible marshes immediately behind the coast. Control of key bridges and cross-roads deeper inland to deny German reinforcements and provide routes for the advancing 4th ID was the responsibility of 82nd AD. They would also blow or control certain bridges farther south for use in further advances or to deny them to the enemy. Where 6th AD had three clearly defined missions supported by four landing zones and two drop zones, American objectives were more numerous and farther inland, therefore harder to locate and accomplish. That resulted in six drop zones and three landing zones (perhaps a legacy of the Knollwood Maneuver?).

A night parachute drop for the bulk of the US force was approved on 22 April with gliders landing at dawn once LZs were secured. Terrain behind Utah favored that tactic, IF the initial paratroop drops were good. Most fields in the area were unfavorable for glider landings. With D-Day approaching fast there was little opportunity for pre-invasion photo recon to troll for 82nd and 101st landing sites.

There were few obvious landmarks; no Orne to help transport pilot orientation in the moonlight, and crossing several minor east-west running rivers could confuse navigation. The Douve, a major north-south water course to the east of the DZs, was wide and straight for six miles inland but couldn't help locating the big paradrops. It was too far east to be seen for most jumps. When it turned west it was easily confused with the north-south running Merderet.

On 6 June the right flank of Neptune began to come unglued almost immediately and got steadily worse. Wary of 'friendly' naval anti-aircraft fire disasters in the Med, troop carrier routes swung wide to the west, going 'feet dry' with uncertain accuracy on an almost featureless coast. Three DZs and one LZ were six to eight minutes flying time inland—plenty of time to get more lost. Ground fog and low clouds made course verification difficult and only four C-47s in ten flew with a Navigator. Radio silence meant crews couldn't warn each other of conditions or ask for help if lost AND, defenders reacted quickly.

Twenty plane-loads of pathfinders went in first, landing clean and correct (within a mile of their objectives in most cases) to guide the main landings but the more than 800 main lift aircraft didn't fare as well. Radios failed and marker beacons set up by pathfinders only worked if troop carrier pilots got within a few miles.

Jumps began just before 0100 on 6 June and 13,000 parachute infantry were off-loaded with another 4,000 men to land in gliders at dawn.

Darkness, dense clouds, high winds, and now alerted German forces putting up flak and small arms fire, served to confuse and scatter some flights of C-47s. Some pilots bored in on their drop targets. Others jinked, veered away, speeded up (beyond safe jump conditions), or went to higher altitude, resulting in badly spread drops and drops into locations far from the ground objectives. Tragically, some C-47s dropped short and troops went into the marshes just behind the beach. Some men drowned before they could shed their chutes and gear.

Overlord commanders had to know where those men were and what were they doing. Despite bad weather PR Spitfires and American F-5s combed the area, collecting aerial imagery inland from Utah Beach, some of which is included below.

The Cotentin Peninsula west of Utah was under solid cloud cover and morning mist/fog was building in the landing areas. Apparently 505th PIR was the only unit that got a really good clean drop (near Sainte-Mere-Eglise).

Below is Drop Zone C, 4,500 feet due west of Sainte-Marie-du-Mont looking south. The chutes are probably from three C-47s. Drops for 101st AD were reported as widely scattered but these chutes are right on the DZ. I only see six or so canisters and no tracks indicating canisters taken away, so the chutes can be assumed used by parachute infantry in their midnight jump. I would expect frames to the right and left to show more chutes from parallel flights of transport aircraft.

On small scale imagery scattered chutes are usually difficult to spot, and aerial photos seldom let a PI see the men, much less what they were doing. But imagery like this reassured staffs in England that most airborne troops were near where they were supposed to be.

Only a small percentage of them actually were. Glider landings were even more scattered. A thousand Wacos and 300 US flown Horsas had a narrow window in time and space to land west of the Douve before German defenses organized and weather closed in.

101st AD.

D-Day, 4,000 feet SW of Sainte-Marie-du-Mont. Probably part of LZ E.

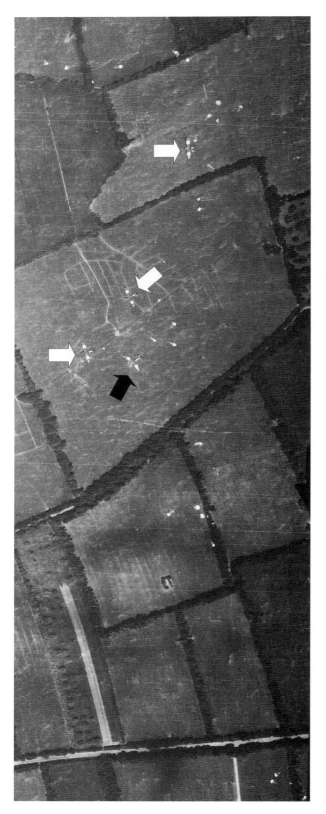

Enlargement and annotation of the previous photo gives a better look at the Wacos and chutes in fields southwest of Sainte-Marie-du-Mont. This is part of the 101st Airborne Division assault.

These glider landings were made from right-to-left.

Deeper inland behind the right flank of Utah Beach the going was tougher for 82nd Airborne. Their mission was to secure roads near Sainte-Mere-Eglise and bridges over the Merderet River (running farther inland and parallel to the ocean) but intense ground fire caused the loss of many transports and a seriously scattered drop. Troopers on the 'wrong side' of the Merderet couldn't join their units. Other men drowned in the Merderet flood-plain or were shot in the air as they descended. Assembly into viable fighting units was slow in the darkness. Ironically, the scattered forces also made it impossible for defenders to determine how many paratroops had landed and what their objectives were.

For many DZs it was 'Indian fighting' as small groups of men crept about in the dark, feeling for the enemy and raising hell.

In spite of impressions in movies and popular anecdotal history, the 82nd secured Sainte-Mere-Eglise by 0430 hours on 6 June.

82nd AD.

Few of the American glider landings went as planned. This is the same field as the previous photo. A mosaic of two 7 June photos of the American LZ southwest of Sainte-Marie-du-Mont shows gliders coming down in close proximity with ones landed earlier. The Horsas appear to have landed left-to-right—in the opposite direction from earlier landings. Additional parachutes, some with canisters still attached, are probably from a subsequent supply drop on this LZ.

That Horsa facing a Waco has lost part of its left wing to an obstruction, perhaps a tree in the hedge behind it. The wreckage next to the tree line is a puzzle (enlargement below). I can only differentiate pieces of one glider. Since there was nothing in that location on the 6 June imagery, and subsequent landings were Horsas, two Horsas colliding on landing is the most logical answer.

This D+1 USAAF right oblique from an F-5 looks south (unfortunately into the sun) at landings 1000 feet NW of Boutteville. The place is called Boutteville Marshes, half way between Sainte-Marie-du-Mont and Sainte-Mere-Eglise. It is the northern fringe of 101st Airborne Division D-Day Drop Zone C. Like many of the others in this book, these fields are still recognizable on Google satellite imagery.

In this example, the choice of a glider landing field was excellent—long, flat, dry, and unobstructed by trees, defenses or hedgerows—a rare occurrence in boccage country. A good LZ contributed a lot to a well-executed landing with few casualties. There are more than 50 chutes on the ground, 25 Horsas, six Wacos and one possible Hamilcar (though I found no record of US use of a Hamilcar). All gliders coming down in or near the same fields demonstrated the advantage of a daylight operation and some excellent pre-Invasion Intelligence work despite the short lead-time.

Enlargement of the Boutteville Marshes glider landing. Skid marks show the direction of landing. A number of chutes from 6 June are on the left. More were in the fields just beyond the upper right of the photo.

Below, an even greater enlargement of the left end of the above image. A few of the chutes show canisters but most were probably from jumpers. It appears the gliders came in from the left (east). Two appear to have damaged wings.

Still looking at the excellent landing NW of Boutteville (this photo is a few feet west of the previous photo). These Horsas landed in daylight on 6 June. The jumpers came in earlier, in the dark. This is the north edge of DZ C.

In spite of a badly broken glider in the hedgerow (left center) and another in the trees (lower right) it looks like everyone else got down safe. Marks on the ground indicate an approach from left to right. I have no idea how the glider got into the hedge like that, it might have struck the hedge before it touched down on the ground. Gliders with the tails off have been opened by their crews to bring out small vehicles such as Jeeps or anti-tank guns.

Roughly 8,000 feet southwest of Sainte-Marie-du-Mont, near Vierville (showing on the road at lower right). North is up and to the right. This is an extension of Drop Zone D, two and a half miles west of the Douve.

Some of these Waco landings appear to have come from the right, others from the left. Perhaps it was two separate landings or a second pass when the first was missed?

German troops were on alert and ground fire may explain why these Wacos have deposited some 300+ glider infantry spread over a mile and a quarter of France, making for slower assembly into a viable force.

Though near pre-planned LZ D this landing is a good example of 'should be elsewhere' but the fields are good and the nineteen Wacos landed well. Six had difficulty, and only three of those look really serious.

I have annotated the previous photo to show gliders I see on the ground in this scattered landing near Vierville on D-Day. White arrows are good landings. Black arrows are damaged gliders.

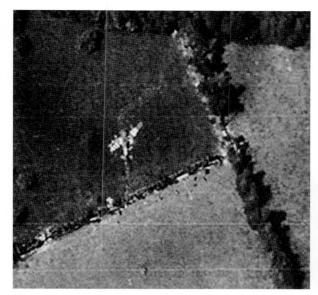

Pilots say 'any landing you can walk away from is a good one.' Once free of the tow-plane, a glider has only one shot and it is moments from touching down. Sometimes options were limited and not all decisions by a harried pilot were good ones.

The enlargements on this page are all from the 6 June 1944 Vierville landings.

Upper left shows no skid marks leading through the hedgerow so the Waco must have actually touched down in the field where it lies with friction stopping it within a few feet (note short track behind it). Stress appears to have snapped both wings but the fuselage is upright.

At right are a good landing and a bad one. Fuselage shadow on the wing and horizontal stabilizer tells me the Waco at lower right is on its back.

Below, the middle Waco of three is missing its right wing (which may be along the hedge to the right). Another crash site at upper left has a badly broken Waco. Invasion recognition stripes usually make it easy to line up wing and fuselage parts but not in this case. It looks like both wings broke off. No skid marks lead to the wreck, suggesting the glider missed the smooth field, diving to a dead stop in the brush.

Six Waco's and a Horsa show the way to land, tight and clean. Skid marks show the distance required for a glider to stop. These are reinforcements for 101st AD. The photo is from D+1. The field is an extension of Landing Zone E, 1500 feet ESE of Boutteville. Chutes in the upper field are likely jumps into DZ C on 6 June

At dawn on 6 June, and over the next few days, all three airborne divisions were reinforced by additional gliders bringing in light vehicles, more troops, light artillery and anti-tank guns. New landings on D+1 helped a build-up in the west to isolate the German stronghold port of Cherbourg. A cellophane tape repaired 7 June photo (below) shows C-47s and Wacos coasting-in just northwest of Utah Beach at low tide. Some off-shore beach defenses, mostly Czech-hedgehogs and posts, can be seen at lower left. Beached landing craft and Allied support ships at Utah Beach are in the distance.

This is probably the 325th Glider Infantry Regiment being delivered to reinforce 82nd Airborne Division at Sainte-Mere-Eglise. Unlike the south-to-north British landings, most of the American drops and landings seem to have been made from the north or west.

This series of negatives were the only images I ran across that showed an actual D-Day combat landing in progress. They were classified RESTRICTED (a security classification no longer used). The number at lower left was the Intelligence File location for subsequent retrieval.

Below, another photo in the same series shows the poor options for landing sites. More than half of the Horsas and Wacos have crashed into tangles of dense hedgerows and tree lined field boundaries. More glider tows are approaching. Despite a better option at upper left, these glider infantry troops got down safely and quickly assembled, joining 4th Infantry Division to bottle up the German garrison in Cherbourg.

Use of Horsas for this reinforcement permitted delivery of vehicles and heavier equipment such as Jeeps and howitzers.

Daylight landing gave a better chance for a glider to get down clean. With US controlling the ground, C-47s circled the LZ, giving glider pilots a better chance to pick a good field. Tow-cable release was usually around 600 feet AGL.

At right are C-47s with Waco tows still attached, other gliders on the ground and one at lower right about to touch down in LZ W.

Another enlargement from the same 7 June photo series. Gliders are circling in a different direction and it seems a crash at lower right caused a fire.

Fields in the center of the photo (arrows) show a series of white dots that may be chutes from a previous paratroop landing, a 6 June night drop, or, more likely, a daylight canister drop with supplies on 6 June.

Troop carrier pilots came in for a lot of criticism following D-Day. The most serious complaints were airspeed too high making jumps dangerous; altitudes too high, making for too long a descent and more vulnerability to ground fire; or altitude too low for parachutes to properly open. Those all resulted in some deaths and more injuries than expected, but most of the under-trained aircrews steadfastly did their jobs as briefed in the face of a first taste of enemy ground fire.

DRAGOON

Two months after D-Day the Allies made a similar airborne and on-shore landing in southern France. Operation Dragoon had three US infantry divisions and the 1st Free French Armored Division landing 200,000 men half way between Marseille and Nice.

On 15 August 1st Airborne Task Force, a new US/UK organization supported the Dragoon landing with battalion and brigade-sized parachute and glider operations. Like the Invasion of Normandy, airborne infantry was first in. The US 509th Parachute Infantry Battalion, 517th Parachute Regiment Combat Team, and British 2nd (Independent) Parachute Brigade were augmented by a glider infantry battalion and a parachute infantry battalion, bringing 1st Airborne Task Force up to about 9,000 men.

Some units landed up to 13 miles from their DZ/LZs, near Le Muy. The airborne force had relatively unopposed landings about nine miles inland from the coast, but gliders suffered badly from 'Rommelspargel'.

Total casualties for Dragoon's air landings numbered just over 400, mostly from the difficult landing conditions.

Dragoon's objective was to convince German forces in southern Europe that they were going to be squeezed between the expanding Normandy lodgment and the new advance. It was hoped they would pull out to the north, freeing southern and central France. That objective was realized in just four weeks.

Chapter VII

AIRBORNE-CENTRIC ASSAULT

Parachute infantry regiments committed in June 1944 fought in Normandy as regular infantry for several months, then went to England for refitting and bringing units back up to strength with replacements.

After Normandy, the Germans thought they knew a lot about Allied airborne capability and how to deal with it. Fully expecting to face the Allied airborne elites again soon, in the fall of 1944 German Intelligence issued a booklet on British and American *Fallschirmjäger*. It appears produced almost entirely from 'open sources' acquired through neutral countries. I doubt any of this was of much value to German soldiers on the ground.

Below, British troops wearing their famous maroon berets and Denison smocks, apparently during a route march training maneuver in England.

Abmarsch von Fallschirmtruppen nach Einsatz bei einem Manöver

The German Intelligence Study included photos of US parachute infantry and glider infantry troops with main and reserve chutes. They also wear the coveted Corcoran 'jump boots'. The photos probably came from American magazines forwarded by German military attachés in neutral countries. Uniforms and gear look like late 1942 or early 1943, i.e., before their first combat use.

Below, more from the German booklet showing British airborne troops training 'with machine-gun, machine-pistols and rifles'. The uniforms are basically copies of those used by German paratroops in 1940–41.

USA. Fallschirm- und Luftlandetruppen

Anlage 10

Fallschirmjäger mit Brust- und Rückenfallschirm und Stahlhelm ... zur Ausführung als Kopfbedeckung

Fallschirmtruppe mit Brust- und Rückenfallschirm und Lederhelm als Kopfbedeckung

(Diese beiden Bilder zeigen wahrscheinlich die gewöhnl. Uniform)

Fallschirmtruppen mit l. MG., Maschinenpistolen und Gewehren

140

Britische Fallschirm- und Luftlandetruppen

Ärmelabzeichen der Fallschirmtruppen
(Kräftig hellblaue Flügel, weißer Fallschirm, alles auf schwarzem Grund)

Ärmelabzeichen der Segelflugzeugführer
und der Artillerie-Beobachter der Heeresfliegerverbände
(Blaßblaue Flügel, goldene Krone und goldener Löwe, ähnlich
wie die sonstigen R.A.F.- Abzeichen)

Enfield rifles and a spilled chute on the ground show these are British parachute infantry in an obviously staged propaganda photo, probably from a live training jump. The padded headgear is a training helmet.

141

MARKET GARDEN

For a month after D-Day the three airborne divisions fought in France as 'straight leg infantry'. When Overlord airborne units disappeared from German Order of Battle maps in July, the Wehrmacht knew they'd probably see them again soon. But, where?

Both sides pondered that. German resistance was stiffening as their Lines of Communication shortened nearer Germany itself, and 36,000 elite infantry were idle in England. The big question for German Army Intelligence was—would the Allied airborne divisions make another air landing or be reintroduced into battle as regular infantry units, as the Germans had done after Crete.

Starting in late August, British Field Marshal Bernard Montgomery pushed for a run around the north end of formidable Siegfried Line defenses, emerging on the North German plain which offered good terrain for maneuver warfare straight east to Berlin. The concept would also isolate German forces in northwestern Netherlands or force them to withdraw.

Armored units would dash north, but they had to cross numerous rivers, canals and streams. If they had to, combat engineers could cope with all but the Maas, Waal and Lower Rhine. Bridging them would cause major delays, allowing enemy forces to adjust and respond. Using lessons of the German Low Country Invasion and Pegasus Bridge, airborne units were assigned the task of securing intact bridges ahead of the advance.

In early September 1944, Operation Comet was planned to take critical bridges at Grave, Nijmegen and Arnhem using British 1st Airborne Division and Polish 1st Independent Parachute Brigade. As subsequent events proved, Comet was seriously understrength for the task (it was officially cancelled on 10 September). Comet was scheduled to launch on 8 September, the same day the German Army began launching V-2 rockets at London from 70 miles west of Arnhem in the Netherlands.

The earlier V-1 barrage on England from France had been blunted by bombing launch sites and destroying weapons in the air, but the flying bomb assault only ended when launch sites were pushed back out of range by Allied ground gains following D-Day. The rocket was more formidable. It was almost impossible to locate launch sites. Nothing could stop a V-2 once launched, and it had a 200 mile range. So, with some urgency, Operation Comet was upgraded and expanded. Dubbed Market Garden, it was locked in largely as conceived with just ten days to prepare for the expansion. Objectives were now to push V-2 launch sites out of range of London, isolate German forces west of the Rhine and free Antwerp (much needed as supply lines lengthened from Normandy). It would also set up a northern drive straight east across good tank country to Berlin (and incidentally make Monty the preeminent field commander ending the war).

American generals opposed shifting emphasis from Eisenhower's Broad-Front Strategy. Lunging north to the Rhine would require reallocation of needed supplies, fuel, transport and reinforcements to Montgomery, virtually ending advances in American sectors.

The plan required an armored dash north from Eindhoven, through Belgium and the Netherlands, to Arnhem. To avoid delay of the ground push it was essential that airborne units would secure key bridges over major canals and rivers before the Germans could blow them. Eight large bridges had to be captured intact. Other minor rivers and canals along the way could be bridged by ground forces if necessary.

It was a 'stove pipe' advance with each force depending upon success of the one to its immediate south. On Day-Four the Guards Armored Division would link up with Britain's 1st Airborne Division at Arnhem Bridge.

MARKET was First Allied Airborne Army landings up to 50 miles behind the FEBA. British 1st AD, Polish 1st Independent Parachute Brigade, US 82nd AD and US 101st AD would secure major bridges along the route of advance. Classic airborne doctrine, it would be a larger assault than Normandy and transport aircraft would go deeper into occupied territory than any earlier airborne assault. Market would be the most ambitious airborne operation in history, with 20,011 troops coming in on chutes and 14,589 by glider. Gliders would bring in 1,736 vehicles and 263 artillery pieces, and 3,342 tons of ammunition and other supplies were subsequently dropped or flown in. Over 1,700 airlift planes would be used, mostly C-47/Dakota transports augmented by converted RAF bombers. Other modified bombers would make supply drops.

GARDEN was a British show with XXX Corps (2nd Household Cav Bde, 5th Guards Armored Bde, 32 Guards Bde, 43rd Wessex ID, 50th Northumbrian ID and 8th Armored Bde) advancing on an axis Eindhoven-Veghel-Nijmegen-Arnhem, thence to the Zuider Zee. Armored units were to progressively link up with and relieve airborne bridgeheads and cross the Rhine.

Market Garden would be a campaign of distances with the final objective (Arnhem) some 50 miles north of the existing Forward Edge of the Battle Area. That was five times deeper behind enemy lines than any previous airborne operation. Some of the airborne landing sites, and XXX Corps main line of advance, would be within a few miles of Germany proper. Unlike Overlord which was based upon optimum moonlight and tides, this operation was based upon urgency. It would take place during dark-of-the-moon, so all landings would be in daylight. Unfortunately haste meant no chance for the detailed planning that made Neptune a success. It was particularly apparent as British 1st Airborne Division, which hadn't participated in Normandy, seemed to ignore most of the lessons learned by 6th AD.

As in Overlord, the majority of USAAF transports carried paratroops on the first day (17 September) and switched to glider tows on the second lift. Most of the 558 RAF aircraft towed gliders. However, on the first day there was only enough airlift capacity for half of the British force and none for the Poles. So the most vulnerable landing, the far northern end of the Garden, would begin with 1st Airborne Division under strength.

Because of Airborne unit vulnerability while landing, surprise was important for success and that meant knowing what you were getting into. Like other operations, planning began with intensive Intelligence gathering. Libraries and intelligence files were combed for information and photoreconnaissance missions were laid on to cover the line of advance. The route was well covered within days but small-scale imagery meant current enemy Order of Battle information was limited. As it turned out, ten days of final Intelligence collection, planning and preparation proved insufficient to cover mission objectives and analyze all the potential landing sites. Chances of the operation succeeding began to narrow.

Looking south at Arnhem Bridge and open land beyond this pre-war photo shows houses on the north end of the bridge: the only locations for several blocks inland overlooking the roadway and commanding access to the structure.

Another pre-war photo, looking north, showed one of two self-powered removable sections of a Rhine River pontoon bridge moved to the side downstream to let a boat pass. Having another way across the river might be important if the pontoon sections could be secured, but on 17 September both center sections had been removed to a location downriver and damaged.

PONTOON B
WITH REMOV
TO PERMIT

Searching for additional ways to get over the Rhine, photo interpreters in England noted the gapped pontoon bridge (right arrow) 2000 feet downriver from Arnhem Bridge. The left arrow indicates where the missing span was parked. Airborne planners hoped to make use of the water-level bridge. Being able to use that bridge was a long shot.

Two other possibilities were a ferry at Driel, about two miles downriver (left), a railroad bridge two miles farther left of this photo and a ferry southwest of Oosterbeek, eight miles downriver from Arnhem Bridge. Once the decision was made to land 1st AD west of Arnhem on the north side of the river, those downriver options became more important.

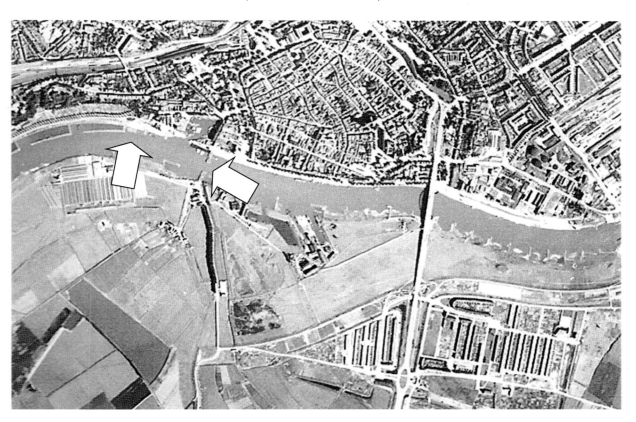

Arnhem's road bridge and wide flood plain on the south bank.

I would have landed there but 1st AD planners deemed the ground too soft for gliders that would bring in most of the force.

Enlargement
US 7PG photo
12 Sept 1944

I used 12 September imagery for this mosaic showing the distance from Arnhem west to Ede (north is to the left).

Here's what 1st AD planned. The long arrow is Arnhem Bridge.

The parachute DZ L is indicated by a shorter thin arrow.

Gliders would land nearer Ede using large open fields on both sides of the rail line (between the lower arrows). LZ S is north of the rail line, LZ Z is south.

DZ X is on the western side of LZ Z and DZ Y is fields about under where a Second World War PI wrote 'EDE' on the neg.

Deelen Airfield is upper left in the middle photo.

I have no doubt the Netherlands Invasion was planned using this imagery.

Deelen Airfield, shown in this enlargement of the previous imagery, figured large in 1st Airborne Division planning because it was one of the few Arnhem-area locations with records of enemy reactions. It had been bombed several times (note craters) and, as all airfields, had anti-aircraft artillery for defense.

Deelen was rail-served by a spur from the Arnhem-Ede mainline. That line, seen heading down and to the right was of major significance after the airborne landings.

Two US 7th PG photos from five days before the invasion show the eleven miles between Nijmegen (bottom) and Arnhem (top) bridges.

A Second World War PI in England circled two items of interest west of Arnhem—the pontoon bridge and, farther left, the Driel Ferry. Between those annotations is a railroad bridge. Arnhem Bridge is farthest right.

Rail and road lines run south to converge at Nijmegen.

There are no hills, valleys, streams or other obstructions between Arnhem and Nijmegen (bottom).

Making that distance looks so easy from 28,000 feet overhead.

Enlargement of 12 September Nijmegen coverage shows the long, multi-span rail (left) and highway (right) bridges over the Waal that would be extremely difficult to replace, particularly under combat conditions—both were over 2,000' long. Either bridge could support tanks crossing to the north bank. Those two bridges were as critical as the one at Arnhem. They had to be secured quickly if XXX Corps tanks were to stream north in relief of 1st Airborne Division eleven miles north.

The light gray area in the town between the bridges is classic fire damage viewed from overhead. RAF and USAAF aircraft accidently bombed here on 22 February 1944, destroying the center of the Netherland's oldest city and killing 800 citizens.

Six miles southeast of the Nijmegen bridges, large, open fields inside the 'U' of a rail line at Groesbeek caught the eye of 82nd AD glider planners. The German border is less than two miles east but a good landing ground was hard to resist.

Meticulous collection of pre-war information provided quite a bit about Arnhem and the route south on short notice. In addition, I have prints from several comprehensive USAAF aerial recce missions (there were doubtless others flown by the RAF) so Market Garden units were hardly going in blind despite the short lead-time.

Pre-Invasion Intelligence collection from September 1944 resulted in three interesting stories that persist as excuses for failure to get over the Lower Rhine.

First: low altitude reconnaissance imagery showing German tanks near Arnhem were disregarded by British commanders. It made an impression in a 'popular history' and movie, but the photos weren't in Intelligence files I culled. Have they ever been published? How could they remain in the dark for so long? I've worked for senior officers who had small regard for Intelligence, but I've never known one who wasn't sensitive to possible changes in enemy Order of Battle. This may be one of those canards that, once published have a life of its own as other authors use the initial reference as a source. Ground truth proves German armored vehicles were indeed present in the area. Many of them were with guns and tracks removed, preparing for rail movement to Germany. I searched all of the rail lines and didn't see them. I believe 9th SS Pz was probably on Deelen Airfield (4.5 miles north of Arnhem), or around Apeldoorn (14 miles north). I didn't find coverage east of Arnhem, the probable location of 10th SS Pz. Small scale limited interpretation—and I'd like to have a better look at the shapes between arrows in the Arnhem rail yard. Normal freight car spacing can be seen in the rail yard to the right. Cars between the arrows could be spaced apart to facilitate end-loading of tracked armored vehicles wider than the railroad flat cars.

Of course German tanks could have moved near Ede, Deelen Airfield or Arnhem after 12 September, but, absent a low oblique or large scale vertical recon photo showing something the easily recognized size and shape of an armored vehicle (tanks being prepared for transit would not likely be camouflaged), I remain skeptical of the story of pre-invasion imagery showing tanks.

Second: Claims that Montgomery dismissed ULTRA intercepts of 16 September indicating movement of the two Panzer Divisions. If true, I think it was simply too late to stop what was in motion for the next morning, and V-2s were dropping on London.

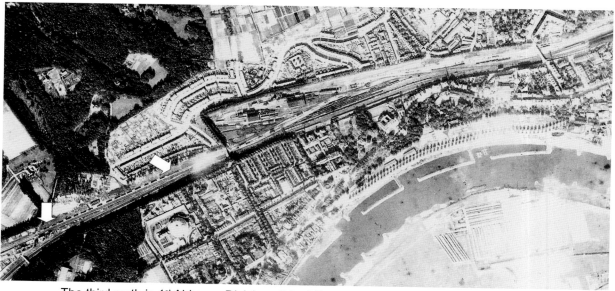

The third myth is 1st Airborne Division glider LZs and parachute DZs were dictated by anti-aircraft defenses near Arnhem, precluding landing closer to the objective. Articles I've read indicate the source of that information was Bomber Command reports of flak. The RAF had attacked Deelen Airfield on several occasions but nothing at Arnhem itself. One would expect to encounter anti-aircraft defenses at an airfield, but that was well out of range for a glider force circling to cross Arnhem from east-to-west. I extensively searched pre-invasion imagery of Arnhem (which was good enough to see anti-aircraft positions) and saw no heavy or medium flak positions south of Arnhem. Screening imagery north of the Rhine was another matter. With the scale and resolution available, flak batteries located in built-up areas would be very hard to spot. AAA guns aren't often positioned in urban areas (except in Flak Towers) because buildings limit fields of fire. Of course there might have been light-flak (automatic weapons) near the bridge. The imagery isn't good enough to see that. LtCol Frost's rapid control of the bridge suggests no German heavy weapons present for several days.

Actually, aircraft going to the 1st AD landing zones were closer to known AAA at Deelen than if they'd landed on the south bank near the bridge. It seems to me British LZs were selected based upon being the largest, open fields in the area; an excess of caution; and defense information more correct for north and west of Arnhem than for Arnhem itself.

Daylight landings for Market meant more exposure to ground fire and faster enemy response to the surprise. On the plus side, it should have meant more accurate, tighter drops and glider landings, and faster unit assembly on the ground.

Parachute troops would go first, securing Landing Zones and holding them for glider landings to bring in supplies, reinforcements and heavier equipment such as vehicles and anti-tank guns.

With only minimal preparation, on the morning of 17 September 1944 the Allies set off to invade Holland with the largest airborne force ever assembled.

Despite being put together quickly, the air movement part of the op was a marvel of organization, pulling together gliders, transports, bombers, aerial reconnaissance and fighters. On the ground, armored and infantry units would have to realign advance axes, shifting fuel and ammunition supplies to the assault forces and assigning tasks to engineers, artillery and logistic forces. The size of this effort boggles the mind. I doubt it could have been put together by planners and commanders before the Normandy Invasion experience provided a model for that level of staff work. American Airborne units assigned had jump and combat experience in Normandy. A critical factor missing was time for combat simulation training of troop carrier air crews.

On Day-One the air space from England to the objectives was filled with waves of aircraft (some on decoy missions to divide enemy air defenses). A thousand fighter planes would ensure control of the air over the battle. Those below are probably USAAF P-47 'Thunderbolts'.

Over 900 bombers would suppress flak, soften and confuse the enemy as to the nature of the effort. Next came 1545 C-47 transports carrying paratroops or towing gliders, plus 321 converted RAF bombers towing gliders.

German radar and ground spotters picked up the inbound flights and pieces of the puzzle began to fall into place in German HQ. It was quickly apparent that where they didn't already have a force on site it was too late to stem the flood of light infantry.

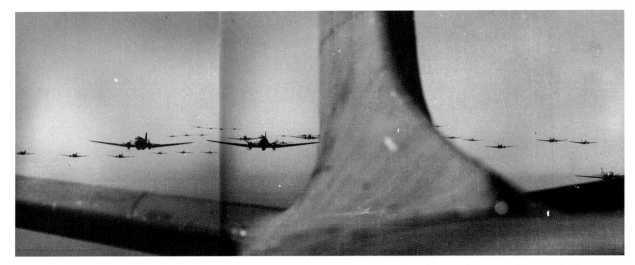

Flying 200 miles deep into enemy territory with concentrated streams of unarmed 'wet-wing' aircraft cruising at 160 knots (150 knots with gliders) was unprecedented. It was only possible because Allied fighters had overwhelming control of the air.

As in Overlord, the first wave for both American airborne divisions was 'jump heavy' with gliders coming later. The British 1st Airborne Division was light on jumpers and heavy on airlanding infantry (gliders). The photo below shows C-47s carrying paratroops on the way to drop zones in Holland. Heavy morning fog in England delayed takeoffs and meant landings in the Netherlands around noon. Many of these planes would be turned around in England to sortie again towing gliders on Day-Two.

Heading for home on 17 September, a USAAF photoreconnaissance plane on a pre-invasion mission imaged inbound C-47s towing Waco CG-4A gliders heading for 325th Glider Infantry Regiment landings at Groesbeek.

154

A second after the previous enlargement, the recce plane caught two overlapping invasion streams sharing the same route into Holland. Six USAAF C-47s and Wacos heading for an 82nd AD LZs are overtaken by five four-engine RAF Short Sterling bombers (in camouflage livery) pulling Horsas bound for the 1st Airborne Division landing at Arnhem. The British are at a slightly higher altitude.

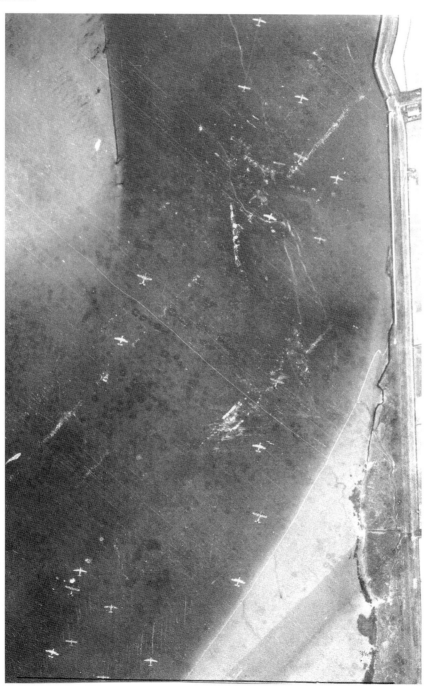

Enlargement of the previous photo shows a camouflaged Short Sterling bomber and its towed Horsa overtaking American C-47s towing Wacos.

Keeping all those routes and all those aircraft sorted out was the job of the radar station at 'Greyfriars' near Dunwich on the coast of East Anglia. Those radars could monitor multiple targets out to 200 miles. The plotting board below shows ingress and egress for the first waves of the Invasion of Holland.

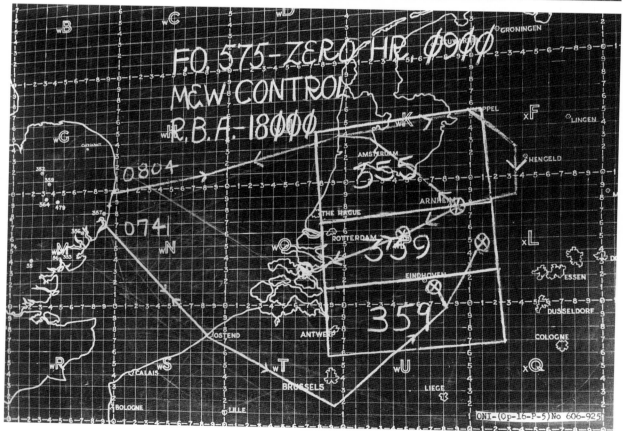

'Greyfriars' was housed in tents, Quonset huts and trailers but the equipment was TOP SECRET and highly sophisticated for its day. Signal collectors were a long-range MEW (Microwave Early Warning) antenna (rear) and a height-finder (foreground). The installation was right on the coast and had no apparent air or ground defenses.

ONI-(Op-16-P-5)No 606-923

-16-P-5)No 606-913

Young men intently watching their radar scopes were some of the busiest troops in England on 17 September 1944. They monitored and helped direct various streams of invasion and diversion aircraft going in and out of European airspace. They were on high alert for indications of any enemy attempt to intervene in the air.

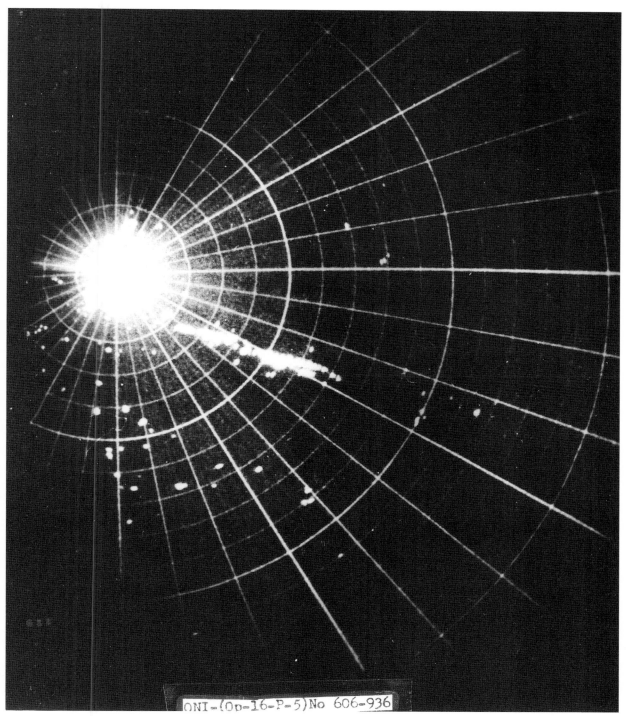

ONI-(Op-16-P-5)No 606-936

Looking out 90 to 100 miles, the air invasion is beginning with Northern and Southern Airborne Armies flying parallel. A stream of aircraft from East Anglia is heading for the Netherlands. Other scattered blips are air patrols, aborting aircraft turning back and reconnaissance flights.

The frisket at the bottom identifies this series of photos as coming from retired files of the Office of Naval Intelligence, Air Intelligence Group (ONI Op-16).

159

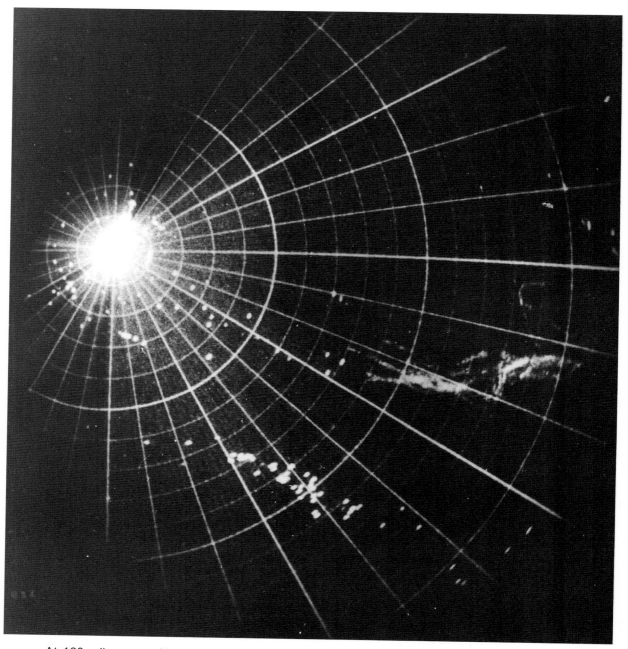

At 160 mile range, Northern and Southern Airborne Armies are turning on their approach courses for separate objectives. Troop carrier planes and gliders are nearing the target areas and dropping chaff ('window,' strips of radar reflective foil) to confuse enemy air defenses. A diversionary bombing force can be seen farther south. Nijmegen is about 190 miles from 'Greyfriars'.

Radar range: 120-200 miles. 'Window' trails show streams of planes in their target areas dispensing chaff. Some of the troop carrier force has completed dropping paratroops and begun to withdraw.

The southernmost leg of Market Garden was assigned to 101st Airborne Division. Their task was to take bridges between Eindhoven and Veghel and they did just that, quickly and efficiently, in part because of excellent selection of DZs close to their individual targets. Stacked from just north of the FEBA to near Son (north of Eindhoven), were 506th PIR, 502nd PIR, and 501st PIR. The northernmost landings for 101st were northwest and south of Veghel.

German reaction was swift but limited by the size of forces available. The Wilhelmina Canal Bridge at Son (just north of Eindhoven) was blown as troopers of 506th PIR approached. The 101st had taken canal bridges at Best, six miles west, so an alternative was available.[13] Engineers working all night successfully restored a bridge at Son, but the ground advance north of Eindhoven was more than a day behind schedule already.

I have never heard or understood why XXX Corps didn't make use of railroad bridges. They had more than enough load capacity to bear tanks.

---

13. Maj.Gen.Maxwell Taylor, 101st AD Commander, saw the advantage of an alternative land route to the west of 'Hell's Highway' but his suggestions weren't heeded by XXX Corps planners.

The 101st Airborne Division's 506th Parachute Infantry Regiment landing north of Eindhoven, 17 September 1944. Nine troop carrier C-47s are seen flying from left to right. Note the typical American low AGL (Above Ground Level) jump altitude to minimize enemy reaction and make the jump tighter to facilitate unit assembly for combat. From plane to ground was a fall of about one minute for the paratroopers.

Unlike the Normandy Invasion night drops, many with bewildering tracers from ground fire, this time troop carrier pilots held to formation, speed and altitude despite ground fire, insuring good landings for the troops.

In some areas German defenses remained active well after the landings. Gliders in an open field near Son, Netherlands. The crashing C-47 was probably shot down during a resupply mission for the 101st AD.

Enlargement shows at least one crewman parachuting to safely (photo center).

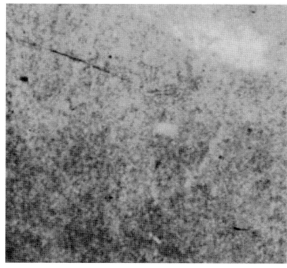

Early German resistance threatened one of the 'Screaming Eagle's' LZs but paratroopers quickly took it back, allowing arrival of the 327th Glider Infantry Regiment (GIR) on 18 September 1944.

Half an hour after the gliders landed, specially configured USAAF B-24s dropped more supplies.

The farm below the road (bottom of the photo) is the same one seen in the vertical photo on the next page.

Chutes and gliders on the ground north of Eindhoven. You can match the square black field and farm on the opposite side of the road to the photo on the previous page.

A few of the gliders on Market Garden imagery had apparently been recovered from Normandy and still wore Invasion recognition stripes but these two (and a few on the next photo) are the only Wacos I ever saw on a combat landing in what was probably the silver paint job as delivered from the factory.

Eight miles northwest of Eindhoven, 502nd PIR was dropped between Best and Sint-Oedenrode and immediately took responsibility for nearby canal and road bridges at both locations. The LZ turned out to be outstanding; good clear fields and just a little over a mile to reach each objective. Other 101st landings were also dead on and all objectives were quickly under control.

There are nearly one hundred 327th Glider Infantry Regiment Wacos on the ground in this photo.

Gliders brought in additional material and men, ensuring capture of all rail and road bridges on XXX Corps route from Eindhoven to those over the Zuid-Willemsvaart Canal and Aa River, extending Allied control farther north to Veghel.

Airborne securing the main land route and its bridges was critical to advance of Garden forces.

Airborne units couldn't hope to guard the entire route, just hold key locations, so British Armored units leading the ground attack were on their own between bridges. Defenders mounted uncoordinated harassing attacks from the north and east. The Germans weren't trying to retake or hold sections of the road, just deny them to the Allies. Even small unit attacks could interdict the tenuous flow of Garden vehicles, fuel and munitions heading north. The road was quickly dubbed 'Hell's Highway' by ground forces.

Garden's route was along a two-lane right-of-way often several feet above the polder country, severely limiting maneuver. Frequently, soft ground beside the road couldn't support the weight of a tank so the advance was pinned to the road, giving defenders an advantage.

This photo is immediately east of the previous shot (north is up and left). The bottom left overlaps the previous photo. I count over 120 Wacos and one Horsa on the ground—and four C-47s (arrows).

In my years of experience, unless the coverage is of an airfield, you seldom see planes on aerial reconnaissance imagery. This is even more unusual because only the one at top right is in the air. Shadows show the other three are on the ground.

These were something I'd never seen before on Second World War Airborne landing imagery. White arrows show C-47s with noses showing more shadow than tails, indicating the 'tail-dragger' planes at top and bottom are sitting on their undercarriage. I doubt these landings were intended.

The black arrow shows a C-47 that appears to be on its back and may have burned.

Curiously, the wrecked plane has a long skid mark and the others don't show any tracks between touch-down and plane. That troubled me at first, then I noticed some of the gliders in the same fields show skid marks and others have none. Clearly this ground had considerable variation in load-bearing capacity. C-47s had fat, low pressure tires and grass field takeoffs and open-field landings were common during Second World War.

Veghel, five miles north of Sint-Oedenrode, on 18 September. On the left is the Zuid-Willemsvaart Kanal and to the right of it the Aa River. Arrows show the four bridges, the upper two are rail, the lower two are roads. Drop Zones of the 501st PIR were to the west (north of the canal) and southwest (south of the canal). These bridges were held by 2nd Battalion, 501st PIR, and 101st AD against an intense two day German counter-attack.

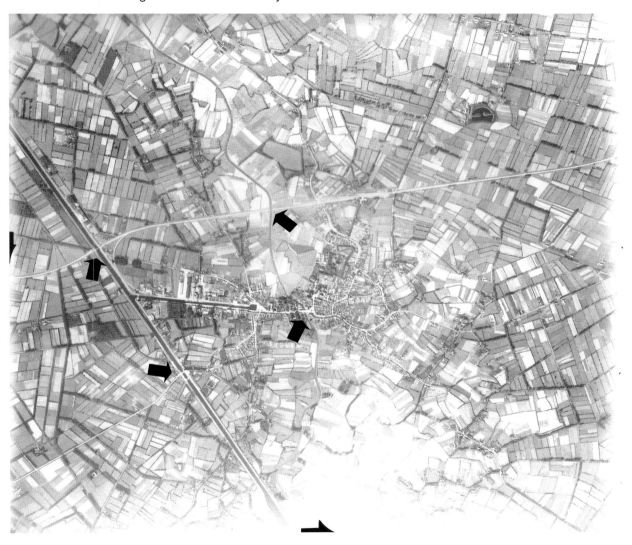

Enlargement of the Veghel coverage is eerie. There is a complete lack of vehicles, movement or signs of battle. Men of the 101st AD are probably already down there and in control, but ground advance delays at Son were being felt. Tanks were supposed to be here at Veghel on Day-One, but they didn't cross these bridges until Day-Two.

Veghel is the northern end of 101st AD responsibility and a little less than half way between Eindhoven and Nijmegen.

Veghel's main road bridge, at the upper end of a canal lock, is indicated by the arrow.

US 82nd Airborne Division was tasked with securing bridges from Nijmegen twelve miles south to Herpen. The major objectives were bridges at Grave and large rail and highway bridges over the Waal at Nijmegen. There were also a number of smaller bridges, most over the north-south running Maas-Waal Canal giving a variety of optional ground routes northeast into Nijmegen proper. The 505th and 508th PIR landed east of the Maas-Waal Canal, southeast of Nijmegen. Southwest of Nijmegen (west of the canal, and north of the Maas) 504th PIR landed near Grave.

My mosaic shows Nijmegen rail and road bridges crossing the Waal River (long arrow) and DZs for 508th PIR (upper right arrow), 505th PIR (lower right arrow) and 504th PIR (left arrow). The water-way divide at bottom center is where the Maas-Waal Canal comes off the Maas River which continues west. The canal heads north for the Waal at Nijmegen.

The 504th was in a good location to advance west, east and northeast. Bridges west and southwest were in reach of 505th PIR. Market Garden's right flank was screened by 508th PIR (the German border is literally feet east) but it turned out to be a poor landing choice for assault on the Waal bridges. Waal bridges, the major division objective, were six miles to the northwest through wooded and urban land (both good defense country). The 508th's major opposition came from the German 2nd Parachute Corps to the east.

Ten miles north of Veghel were three bridges over a small river (the Hertogswetering). The left arrow is a road, center is a railroad bridge and the far right is a major artery leading toward Nijmegen. Either could be used by XXX Corps if captured intact.

Two miles north of Herpen were Maas crossings at Ravenstein/Niftrik. The rail bridge (left) is standing. The road to the right is unconnected. If there was a bridge there, I see no sign of the structure. If it was a ferry, there is no sign of that either. Wijchen, just up the road to the northeast, was the site of sharp fighting by 504th PIR to secure the route to Nijmegen.

Five miles east of here was the preferred route, the bridge at Grave.

The Maas was 450 feet wide but Grave's 1,706 foot, nine-span arched steel truss bridge was the longest in Europe at the time (because of bridging approaches over a wide Maas flood plain). The two bridges at Nijmegen were only slightly shorter. All three objectives were supposed to be taken by Day-Three so land forces could relieve British paratroops at Arnhem on Day-Five.

That is a long time for lightly armed airborne forces to hold ground alone against two crippled armored units. The Grave bridge was actually taken quickly by a Platoon of the 504th jumping just south of the Maas west of Grave. German defenses were still active in Grave city, three-quarters of a mile east, when the rest of 504th PIR jumped and/or airlanded just north of the river.

A caption said this was 82nd Airborne jumping at Grave, but parachute infantry usually went in first. In this case gliders are already on the ground, the aircraft are almost in line formation and the AGL is high. I suspect this is actually a supply drop. I have also seen a photo at this exact same location taken seconds later identified as an Operation Varsity drop. Can't always trust those captions.

Waco gliders of 325th GIR on the north bank of the Maas, just opposite the town of Grave (photo courtesy of Hans den Brok). The gliders are spread out over a large area but all got down safely, though one has a broken right wing.

Ferry piers are on both banks but no ferry is in position. A possible ferry is against the north bank of the 'Y' shaped inlet just downstream. The long bridge, the primary objective, is just 1500 feet to the upper left. Apparently all parachutes had been 'policed up' when this photo was taken on 23 September.

There are no signs of activity. No vehicles on the roads. No smoke from chimneys. Apparently the war has passed on to the north and local citizens are hunkered down, hoping for the best.

Two important bridges south of Nijmegen and north of Grave were where the Maas-Waal Canal began. The rail bridge on the right was a useable asset but the canal-lock bridge at Mook/Heumen (left arrow) was critical to linkage between the 505th PIR (landed off the right side of the image) and 504th PIR (landed just off the lower left of the image).

Both bridges were captured intact on Day-One of the invasion by units of 82nd Airborne Division.

Two miles southwest of the critical Nijmegen bridges over the Maas were four bridges over the Maas-Waal Canal at de Kamp. From the left are a road bridge (out), parallel rail and road bridges (rail intact, road probably intact), and a secondary road bridge at right (out). The route north of Grave led here and getting armor east of the Maas-Waal Canal was vital for expeditiously crossing the Waal itself. These bridges provided XXX Corps with alternate routes to the center of the city if resistance blocked the preferred advance.

DZ N southeast of Nijmegen near Grafwegen. Fields are filled with chutes of the 82nd Airborne's 505th Parachute Infantry Regiment landings and scattered gliders of the 325th Glider Infantry Regiment.

Not far north of here two platoons of 505th PIR held off an attack by three German infantry battalions supported by tanks.

LZ N was more to the east (to the upper right corner of this image). Most gliders heading for LZ O (west of Heumen) on 17–18 September actually landed here.

The initial 82nd Airborne Division's 505th PIR's parachute landing is indicated by the white arrow (on the left). Waco gliders appear badly scattered within the triangle of black arrows but it is a little more than a mile between arrows.

Given the fields available, landings by the 82nd AD were near-perfect and they quickly commanded the high ground between Groesbeek and Nijmegen, but they had to face determined German counter-attacks from the east that occupied their attention and manpower. The Nijmegen Bridge had to wait.

On 20 September the main German attack in this area hit 505th PIR at Mook, just west of this photo.

Immediately east of Breedeweg, 18 September photo. Threading the space between houses lining the roads, 38 Horsas landed within a 2,000 foot radius, bringing in the Airborne Corps HQ and Corps CO LtGen Frederick Browning. Legend says Browning went a mile east to the Reichswald to urinate into Germany, then returned to his HQ and the war. Given the range and unreliability of contemporary radio communications, arrival of the Airborne Corps HQ was a waste of airlift capacity. Browning had no way to find out where his Corps assets were, much less control them. All he could do was pester 82nd AD Commander, MGen Gavin, who had no more information about two of his three parachute infantry regiments. With a glider shortage, those used for Browning and his staff would have been better used sending 1000 more combat troops to 1st Air Division at Arnhem.

Light construction, Spartan instruments and dual controls of a Waco CG-4A. But the pilot had an excellent field of vision to pick his landing spot. This glider, piloted by F/O Dana Mudd, landed at Groesbeek on the 17th and was photographed by a Dutch civilian.

Roughly a mile north, 82nd AD's 508th PIR landed near Groesbeek (remember the area from pre-invasion reconnaissance a few pages back). Look for gliders inside the 'U' of rail line. That bend in the railroad was heading towards the Groesbeek forest and a storage area for munitions. Village people called it the 'bomb-line'. The railroad running to the right top of the photo is heading towards Kleve in Germany, bisecting DZ/LZ N and DZ/LZ T.

The 508th PIR was responsible for defending against a German attack from the east and gaining control of Nijmegen's road bridge over the Waal. That was too much tasking for the force assigned. It accomplished the first mission well but faltered on the second. Landing too far away, when 508th troopers finally fought their way to the bridge, both ends were firmly in German hands.

As at Arnhem, the 82nd had to leave a substantial force to hold the LZ/DZ for landings and supply drops the next day. They also had to take the high ground towards the city and hold it against German counter-attacks. The high ground was deemed most important for control of the entire area, including the Nijmegen Bridge.

Photo Recon on the 17th shows Waco gliders down together inside the rail curve east of Groesbeek. More Wacos and Horsas are scattered in fields farther to the east, beyond this enlargement. Gliders landing around Groesbeek brought in the artillery units, Jeeps, medical and engineers for the 82nd AD.

Forward elements of XXX Corps advanced through Grave early on the 19th and were in Nijmegen that afternoon, but the nearly half-mile long Nijmegen Bridge wasn't in Allied hands for another day.

The next six photos were taken by Jaap Baijnes, son of a Groesbeek doctor. This is the IX Troop Carrier Command taking 508th PIR to DZ T on 17 September 1944.[14]

The combat jump at DZ T.

14. Once again, thanks to Pastor F.G. Thuring of Groesbeek for these pictures taken by a Dutch civilian.

More of the 508th jump at Groesbeek. The AGL of this drop seemed a little high to me. Clearly the planes were expecting ground fire and wanted to get above the effective range of automatic weapons. Unfortunately that made the paratroops vulnerable to the same automatic weapons fire longer.

Another shot of the DZ T jump. Smoke at the right is from a crashed C-47.

Dutch civilians examine a glider near Groesbeek. This glider landed on DZ O on 18 September. The entire 44th Troop Carrier Squadron dropped their 20 gliders in this area. It was a mistake and short of the intended Groesbeek landing zones. This was just one of the misdrops in the 82nd area. Some gliders overshot LZ T and landed in Germany. Most of those men made it back. Another group landed south of the Reichswald. Again, most of them made it to American lines. Nine gliders landed about 11 miles in Germany, all became PoW.

Although the 18 September glider landing at LZ O was a mistake, these fields were used for the 23 September glider lift of the 325th GIR.

One hundred thirty-four B-24s from five Bomb Groups dropped supplies on 18 September. These planes became separated from their main group and dropped on DZ O instead on DZ N in support of 82nd Airborne Division's 505th PIR.

The photo caption said this is 82nd Airborne landing near Nijmegen, making it the 508th PIR north of Groesbeek. Great photo but I'm suspicious. Formation doesn't match the Thuring photos and the AGL seems high—and who was on the ground to take the picture?

Below, chutes on the ground south of Groesbeek prove the 508th jump was tight.

While 508th PIR was occupied fending off German counter-attacks from the east, German forces gathered to maintain control of the Waal bridges. With no Allied troops between the Rhine and Waal, defenders were free to feed reinforcements in from the north.

Market Garden was now two full days behind schedule. Tanks had reached the south bank and fired in support as a company of 82nd AD's 307th Engineer Bn ferried 3rd Bn, 504th PIR over the Waal in small wood and canvas boats provided by the British. It was a courageous but costly five-trip assault crossing. German defenders were laying down heavy fire from behind the dike and an old Dutch frontier fort (small white arrow). US paratroops swiftly followed the route shown by black arrows. When it was obvious they were outflanked, German defenders withdrew from both ends of the road bridge.

Unfortunately XXX Corps then refueled, rearmed and rested for 19 hours before advancing. By 18:30 hours on 20 September the land advance was again underway—but Garden was now too far behind schedule to save 1st Airborne Division at Arnhem.

I can't help thinking if 82nd AD had landed even a small force in the open fields north of the Waal (large white arrow) 4000 feet from the road bridge, they might have taken in a rush on Day-One like at Grave. Was Arnhem or Nijmegen 'the Bridge Too Far'?

Three days into Operation Market Garden the schedule was running seriously behind and the road ahead promised worse. German defenders now knew exactly where XXX Corps was going and set up blocking positions. In some places the road north of Nijmegen was 10 to 15 feet above the surrounding fields so there was no way to maneuver. With no place to go, damaged tanks had to be pushed over the side of the road as XXX Corps struggled north. The British 1st Airborne Division was dangling in the breeze, holding on grit.

Taking and holding the Rhine road bridge at Arnhem was the job of the as yet untried British 1st Airborne Division and Polish 1st Independent Parachute Brigade.

By coincidence, heavy opposition near Arnhem came from two Normandy-battered, undermanned and underequipped Panzer Divisions (9th and 10th SS) resting north and east of Arnhem respectively. Tracked vehicles preparing for rail movement to Germany were hastily returned to combat-ready status. However, each Division had about 7,000 men and two Panzergrenadier regiments able to deploy quickly in response to British landings.

Hours before Market Garden launched, its command and staff may have had Intelligence indicating panzers were present but apparently motion in progress and the barrage of V-2s on London trumped everything.

Weather delayed take-offs so British 1st Airborne landed at 1330 hours with less than half the force assigned to the mission, counting on additional lifts over the next three days to bring the Division up to strength with reinforcements, heavy weapons and supplies.

Below is a field west of Arnhem 1st AD's 21st Independent Parachute Company (pathfinders) marked as a DZ for arriving parachute infantry brigades.

The same field shortly after one of 1st Airborne Division's parachute brigades arrived. It was a good tight drop.

The main force landing was farther west, nearer Ede. I count 226 gliders on this 18 September 1944 photo, most of them Horsas. Skid marks on this enlargement indicate landings from both east and west in the LZ north of the tracks, probably from different waves of glider landings (1st and 2nd lifts). Gliders south of the tracks (photo bottom) all seem to have come from the south, heading north.

Fields selected as LZs for gliders were perfect—large, flat and free of obstructions, easily accommodating the large number of gliders to come.

However, the distance was too great for a rush from landing-to-objective. Troops here were tied up defending the LZs for arrival of subsequent lifts bringing the rest of the Division so they could offer no support to those at the bridge. If sufficient transport aircraft couldn't get through with more glider landings, and if the relieving XXX Corps stalled on the road south, troopers fighting at the bridge would be isolated, out-numbered and on their own.

Unfortunately, all those things happened. The price of a divided lift proved too high.

I put three photos together to show the British 1st Airborne DZ/LZs, late 17 September. North is to the left. More than 220 gliders are on the ground in this mosaic and there were many more just to the north and south. The precision of these landings is remarkable. Pilots came down right where they were supposed to on both sides of the rail line. Too bad they weren't sent closer to the Arnhem Bridge.

Match field patterns at lower right in the mosaic's top photo to see where the paratroops were in relation to the gliders. Arnhem Bridge is 5.5 miles beyond the top of this mosaic.

Two battalions held the LZs while troops of 2nd Parachute Battalion under Lt.Col. John Frost sped into town, expecting to take and hold the bridge until reinforced. Following a route along the river, Frost and his men found the bridge unguarded and took up positions in houses alongside bridge approaches.

German resistance on the ground stiffened rapidly and flak defenses built up in the area over the next two days. British paratroops blocked access to the bridge the night of the 17th but didn't control it.

Weather-delayed landings for 1st AD meant that Germans were aware of earlier 82nd AD landings at Nijmegen, but initially didn't realize another airborne division landing was in progress just west of them that afternoon. Well into the afternoon German defenders didn't know about Frost's men at the bridge and thought their task was to bottle up landings to the south and the new landing reported near Ede.

Shortly after landings on the 17th, but before British paratroops reached the bridge, a 9th SS Panzer column of 40 armored reconnaissance cars and half-tracks rushed south across Arnhem Bridge to scout Allied landings at Nijmegen. Their parent unit was north of Arnhem, probably on or near the rail line at Deelen Airfield, preparing equipment to go to Germany for a refit.

1st AD.

191

Finding they weren't needed at Nijmegen, the German column turned back to Arnhem. By then Frost's men had established control of buildings dominating the north end of the bridge. Frost's troopers destroyed half of the returning SS Reconnaissance Battalion on 18 September. This aerial photo shows the wreckage of SS Hauptsturmführer Gräbner's vehicles blocking the roadway on the north end of the bridge.

An RAF photo reconnaissance Spitfire streaked low over Arnhem to get this oblique showing the wreckage of German vehicles fouling the bridge. Some of those were wheeled armored vehicles but at this point neither 9th nor 10th Panzer could yet deploy their depleted tank regiments, self-propelled artillery guns, battalions of assault guns or anti-tank battalions—all of which seriously out-gunned the British paratroops.

Meanwhile, 1st Airborne Division's 1st and 3rd Parachute Battalions left the glider LZs and tried to push through to reinforce Frost, one advancing beside the railway and the other going straight through the town. Both were stopped by 9th SS Panzer Grenadiers. Heavy infantry and armored reconnaissance vehicles from 10th SS were on the way from the east.

Jeep and backpack radios were either failing or out of range. The SCR-536 (WalkieTalkie) had a one mile range so Frost couldn't talk to the LZ. Jeep or backpack mounted SCR-694 had a 15 mile range. Those and other similar radios used vacuum tubes and many weren't robust enough for glider landings.

The 740 man British force holding Arnhem Bridge was isolated and out of touch.

This is the main LZ, showing more gliders are on the ground. German flak and automatic weapons concentrating nearby made use of this landing zone increasingly problematic for introduction of reinforcements and supplies. The Third Lift and following Supply missions were savaged by ground fire, meaning the body of 1st AD was as cut off from support from England as Frost was cut off from them.

LTC Frost and his men still held the bridge on Day-Four of Market Garden.

Meanwhile, delays taking the bridge at Nijmegen and delays for XXX tanks to push north doomed 1st AD. German tanks and Self Propelled guns had their tracks reinstalled and were in play; 9th Panzer from the north and 10th Panzer from the east. By September 20th air resupply flight paths and drop locations were too predictable, making them extremely hazardous. The Luftwaffe put in an appearance, shooting down a number of converted bombers and C-47s trying to drop food and munitions to the beleaguered 1st Airborne Division.

Confusion, a changing situation on the ground and poor communications with each other and with troop carrier aircraft resulted in many supplies falling into German hands or the river.

This dramatic photo had nothing to identify location or date beyond 'Arnhem' but comparison of fields in the distance with maps and other imagery suggests this is DZ X looking south toward the Lower Rhine. That makes the aircraft approach south-to-north.

The drop seems tight but an unusually high AGL causes me to suspect this may be one of the last 1st AD drops with troop carrier pilots concerned about ground fire.

On 18 September gliders landed the anti-tank battery of Polish 1st Independent Parachute Brigade at Oosterbeek to reinforce 1st Air Division. The next day the light artillery battery glider-landed on the south bank opposite Oosterbeek. Weather delays kept the main body of Polish paratroops on the ground in England.

On Day-Four nearly 1000 Polish paratroops were finally dropped south of the Rhine at Driel. Ground action by the Poles, and the threat they posed to both Arnhem and the retreat route for German forces farther south, tied up thousands of Wehrmacht resources and allowed remnants of 1st Airborne to survive another day.

Polish Parachute Brigade

We know exactly where this photo is. Compare with my mosaic on page 147—the triangle field with an angled farm building just above the lower right arrow on the mosaic are the same features seen at upper left on this photo. That puts this 1st AD parachute drop of supplies on the east edge of LZ Z with aircraft flying south-to-north. Looks like a drop altitude around the usual 600 feet.

There are six gliders on the ground from landings the day before, and eleven C-47s in the air. I won't even attempt to count the parachutes.

A last look at 1ˢᵗ AD LZs no longer reachable by reinforcements from England. Now 1ˢᵗ AD was isolated and its force divided, being pressed south against the river. Mounting German pressure cut off blocking forces from the landing zones on the 19ᵗʰ. North is up.

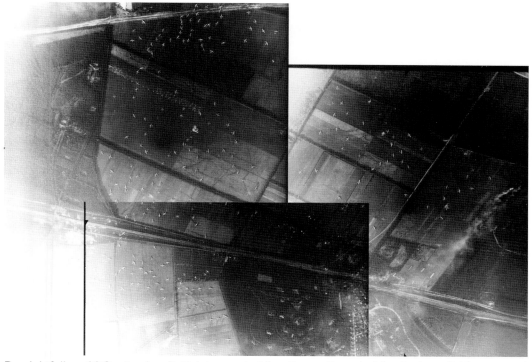

By nightfall on 20 September British troops holding the north end of the Arnhem Bridge ran out of ammunition and were either killed or captured.[15] The rest of 1ˢᵗ Airborne, nearer the landing grounds, were also cut off from the LZ and reinforcement, squeezed into a smaller and smaller area, fighting a rear-guard action, being pressed into Oosterbeek. When the Polish Brigade finally jumped at Driel on 21 September both ends of Arnhem Bridge were in German hands and 10ᵗʰ SS Pz was pressing the new landing hard. The ferry was gone and the north bank heavily defended, so there was no way to cross the river and reinforce remnants of 1ˢᵗ Airborne.

Tanks of XXX Corps, led by the Guards Armoured Division, were finally beyond Nijmegen and pushing north but unable to punch through to Arnhem.

By 24 September XXX Corps tanks had advanced far enough to link up with the Poles, but it was obvious they weren't going to take Arnhem Bridge or cross the river so it was decided to withdraw what was left of 1ˢᵗ Airborne.

Men of 1ˢᵗ AD had held out for nine days. Only 2,000 of the original 10,000 were able to retreat south over the Rhine. By 25 September Market Garden was over. It hadn't put a viable force across the river, nor did it stop the V-2s landing in England or open Antwerp for Allied use, but it did set up positioning of forces that led to the Battle of the Bulge three months later. In that bitter December 1944 struggle 82ⁿᵈ AD, 101ˢᵗ AD, 3ʳᵈ and 9ᵗʰ *Fallschirmjäger* fought as regular infantry.

---

15. In honor of the gallant British stand, in 1978 the rebuilt road bridge at Arnhem was renamed the John Frost Bridge.

LTC Frost and his men held out in those gutted buildings at upper left.

By way of an epilogue, in October, Allied High Command decided if they couldn't use the Arnhem Bridge neither would the Germans. The bridge was bombed on 6 October, with medium bombers missing rather badly.

'Heavies' bombed the bridge the following day with better results.

Two spans were dropped, and nothing was left of the houses around the north end.

Chapter VIII

FAR EAST AGAIN

In late winter of 1944, General of the Armies Douglas MacArthur was steadily making good his pledge to return to the Philippines. He was closing in on Manila (which wouldn't be completely liberated until 3 March) and needed access to Manila Bay to improve logistics for the remainder of the Leyte campaign.

For fifty years the Bay had been defended by formidable concrete forts built by American engineers. Japanese presence in those forts was uncertain, as was the condition of heavy guns and mortars surrendered in 1942. Retaking the forts would open the Bay.

Some resistance was expected but Manila Bay defenses were designed for 1900–1920 warfare using the best techniques, materials and guns of that era. They were not expected to be 'tough nuts to crack' for modern weapons and forces.

Bataan Peninsula is on the left and Manila is at upper right. My annotations below show the fortified islands guarding the entrance to one of the world's greatest anchorages. From north to south: the largest was Corregidor (Fort Mills), nearby Caballo (Fort Hughes), El Fraile (Fort Drum) close to the middle of the passage, and Carabao (Fort Frank) near the south coast and guarding the southern passage. The photo below was taken in 1944 by a 6th Photo Group F-4 (early photo version of P-38) flying from China.

A fifth fort, Fort Wint, guarding Subic Bay and the Naval Base at Olongapo (20 miles NW on Bataan Peninsula), was reoccupied on 30 January 1945.

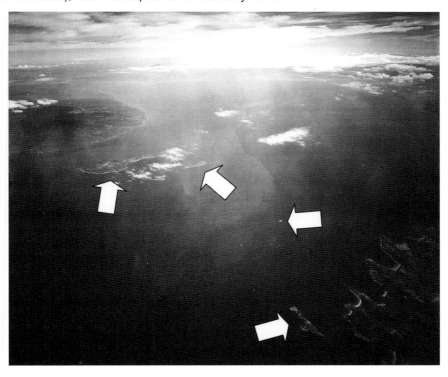

Intelligence may have been spotty about the strength and capabilities of these forts after years of Japanese occupation, but aerial reconnaissance suggested nothing had been done to maintain or improve the basically First World War-style positions and weapons. 'Disappearing Guns' that fired and fell back behind their walls and large mortars in open pits behind concrete walls were adequate to duel with early 1900s warships but hopelessly vulnerable to high angle fire and air attack. This gun is on Fort Frank, after capture in 1945.

With 23 heavy batteries, Fort Mills (Corregidor) had the most defense guns, but like Frank and Hughes, they were in open pits. Below, 12" mortars in Battery Way (shown after recapture) had a range of over eight miles and fired in defense of Bataan in 1942. One of them was the last heavy artillery fired as the Japanese took Corregidor. The Japanese never expected to defend Corregidor and there was little evidence that they maintained the guns but, just in case, they were neutralized by air attack in early 1945.

One fort was a particular concern: Fort Drum. Recognizing its ideal location near the center of Manila Bay's entrance, between the two World Wars US Army Engineers had completely changed tiny El Fraile Island (right), blasting their way deep into the rock below sea level to create an unsinkable battleship.

The new fort mounted four 14" naval rifles in two armored turrets protected by concrete up to 35 feet thick. Facing west toward the South China Sea, its batteries couldn't be trained to the east to threaten anything already inside the bay, or support the defense of Manila, but they commanded the Channels from Bataan to the south coast and could challenge any ship approaching from the west. Drum also mounted four 6" guns and three 3" guns for air and mine-field defense and all of its guns appeared operational. The photo below shows Drum while still in American hands in 1941. A battleship-type fire-control mast was installed along with water and fuel tanks and a wooden superstructure for offices and quarters. The guns of the lower battery can just be seen on the left and the top of the upper turret shows above it.

In 1945 Fort Drum was subjected to intense attack by Allied air in an attempt to neutralize it, but, while the superstructure was bombed away, the only damage to the turrets was destruction of the right barrel on the lower turret.

Drum was manned by 65 Japanese who retreated into the bowels of the fort and wouldn't surrender, even after their big guns and secondary batteries were essentially useless. Finally, on 13 April 1945, a mixture of 3,000 gallons of gas and diesel was pumped into the air shafts and ignited, killing all the defenders. It was the next to last fort to fall.

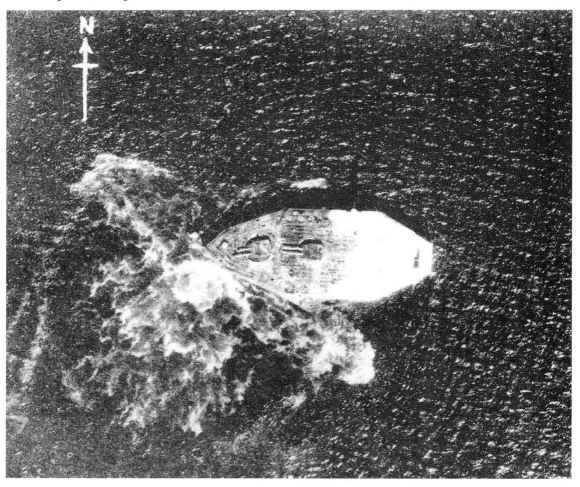

Three days after Fort Drum was destroyed, the final fort, Fort Frank, was invaded and found undefended, thus opening the South Channel into Manila Bay. Fort Hughes had been taken by assault from the sea on 27 March.

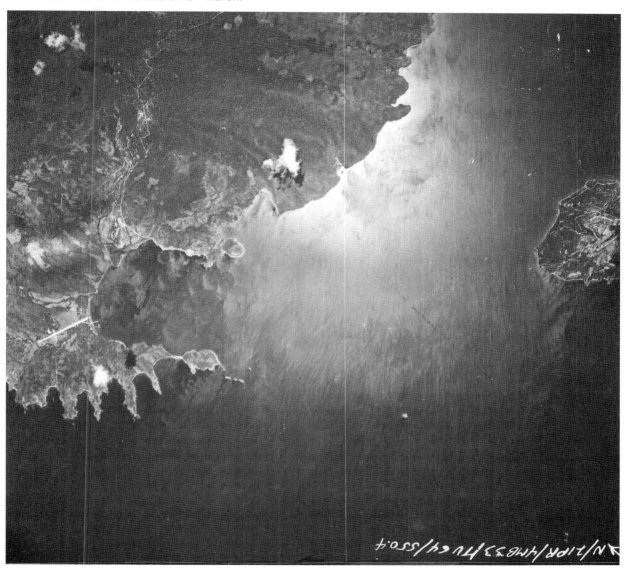

But Corregidor was number one on the priority list.

Of the four Manila Bay forts, Fort Mills was the largest and considered the most important. It was also the biggest question mark. How well was it defended in 1945, and by how many Japanese? Before the Japanese invasion of the Philippines it was considered the strongest fortress in the Pacific, so Fort Mills was in line for recapture immediately after taking Fort Wint secured the left flank of Manila Bay. The photo below is from a 21st Photo Squadron F-4 based in China in May 1944. Bataan is on the left with Mariveles at the upper left of the large bay. Corregidor's high ground is at the right.

Of course Allied Intelligence had access to people who could minutely identify where everything had been in 1942—even so, they misidentified the hospital and warehouses as barracks area on this graphic and didn't name the main barracks and parade ground (under the annotation 'telephone exchange'). That open area and the golf course (near the annotation 'pool') were where paratroops were to land.

'Bottomside,' the lower part of the island, is the narrow isthmus to the right. To the right of 'South Wharf' is Malinta Hill, site of the famous Malinta Tunnel which housed MacArthur and his staff during the Japanese attacks in 1942.

Fort Mills had a variety of guns but the heavy coastal artillery batteries were mainly 10" and 12" guns of 1910–21 vintage. Though old they were still potentially quite dangerous and most were sited to fire in an arc from west to south, toward ships approaching the Bay. On the pre-invasion annotated mosaic, and imagery after American bombing had begun (above), some of the positions appear occupied—but were they operational? Some guns were destroyed during the Japanese attack in 1942 and never repaired; others were subsequently removed by the Japanese for use elsewhere.

Ruins of 'Topside' buildings show damage from the Japanese bombardment in 1942 as well as American shelling and bombing in 1945. Need for a winding road at right leading down to the low ground of 'Bottomside' shows the elevation difference. Battery Crockett is at bottom center. At lower center, the cleared area pock-marked with craters is the old golf course, one of the DZs selected for the parachute assault.

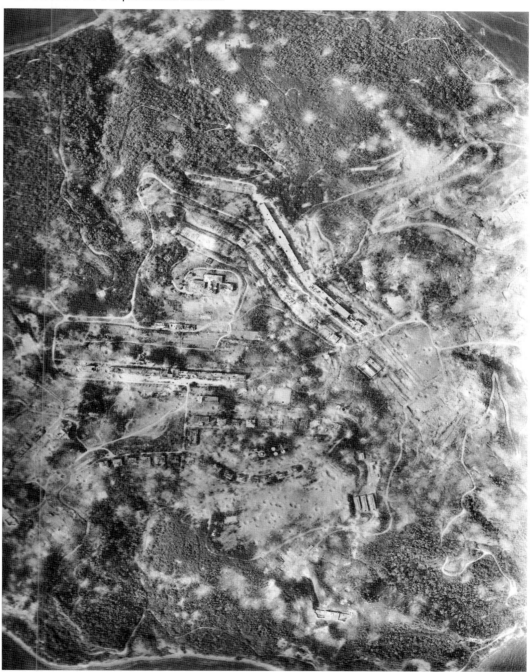

207

Pre-invasion softening up didn't seem to concentrate on the old gun batteries, though it did insure several were out of action. Below is an enlargement of Battery Crockett on Corregidor's south coast. The shadows are deceiving. Those two roughly triangular shapes are concrete pits with higher ground between them and toward the sea (bottom of the photo). Shadows show the walls behind which two 12" guns would hide between firings. Unfortunately the battery faced south and the Japanese attacked from Bataan to the north. Crewed by 30 men, those guns could throw a 900 lb. projectile up to 16 miles with considerable accuracy.

Put out of action in 1942, the Japanese had American PoWs cannibalize from similar weapons on Corregidor to get one of Crockett's guns back in operation. In 1945, since the Allied fleet would come from the south and southwest, if this battery had active guns it might get off a few rounds. But, from that exposed position its life expediency would have been brief.

The gun on the right seems to be intact (sitting atop the circular base that let it traverse), but a hole in the deck behind the gun shows penetration of its 'bomb proof'. Built under the gun platform to store powder bags and projectiles for the gun, the bomb proof was thought to be impenetrable because of the angles of fire required to hit it. It looks like a hit by a bomb, or high-angle fire naval shell, that probably also knocked that gun barrel out of action. I can't see the traversing mount on the left gun position.

Crockett's guns were part of 'the Rock' for forty years, went through two assaults, and never fired a shot in anger.

Another enlargement from the same imagery (**below**) shows damage to Topside facilities. The hospital is at the top. The long narrow building near photo center is the main barracks and the gently curving line of individual buildings is pre-war officer's quarters. Between those last two is the parade ground, one of the parachute DZs and location of the final photos in this series on Corregidor.

Many of the roofs are gone and you can look down inside some buildings. The Japanese didn't bother to rebuild the island's infrastructure or defenses so some of the destruction dates from 1942. That apparent lack of interest caused Allied Intelligence to estimate there were about 600 Japanese on the island in January 1945.

Japanese sources say there were closer to 6,700—only a handful survived US troops retaking the island.

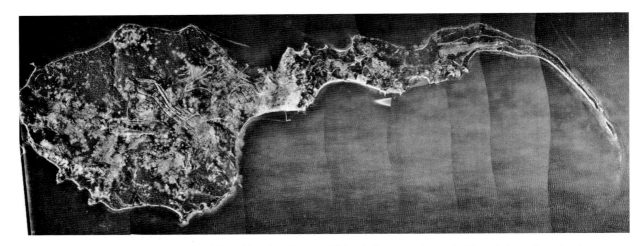

Above is an overview of the objective General MacArthur most wanted to retake—the place he was chased out of in March 1942. This mosaic is from 25th Photo Squadron imagery flown from a base in Leyte on 12 February 1945 (three days before the assault). It was likely used in last minute invasion decisions. The island is three miles long and one and one half miles at the widest point. High ground of 'Topside' is to the left, sloping down through 'Middleside' to the low-lying, light colored area (and the rest of the island) known as 'Bottomside'. The start of 'Bottomside' was the site of North and South Docks (north is up) as well as the little town of San Jose, warehouses and tunnel entrances. Just to the right of the wharfs is high ground of Malinta Hill. In 1942 the area to the right, beyond Malinta Hill, was devoted to Army Air Corps and US Navy functions—barracks, hangers for Kindley Landing Field, and Navy SIGINT radio intercept facilities at Monkey Point (just below the air strip).

Sharp eyes will spot bombs exploding on the north end (far left) of the island.

RETAKING 'THE ROCK'
This oblique looks across the island toward the west and dates from late January 1945. Kindley Air Field is in the foreground. Smoke on 'Topside' indicates softening-up for the invasion has begun. All the facilities on 'Bottomside' around Kindley Field are gone and 'Topside' buildings appear derelict—you can see right through some of the large multi-storied barracks and warehouses.

Another January oblique looks north toward Bataan Peninsula showing serious bombing or shelling around Battery Cheney. The assault plan was to take Japanese defenders by surprise with an air-drop of 503rd Parachute Regimental Combat Team (PRCT) on 'Topside' followed by amphibious landing of 34th Infantry Regiment (24th Inf Div) on both north and south coasts of 'Bottomside'. Those paratroops were the same unit that began Pacific airborne operations at Nadzab.

Surviving Japanese defenders would be squeezed into the narrowing tail of the island by the two forces. Here is where the rationale for this operation starts to get muddy. The landing targets, the parade ground between the old barracks and pre-war officer's housing, and the golf course behind officers housing, were both quite small and subject to powerful cross-winds.

The once-formidable coastal batteries were almost all neutralized by pre-invasion bombardment, though several rounds were fired at ships the day before the attack. The shots were most likely from a Japanese mobile light field artillery piece, not one of old guns.

Aerial photos and visual observation showed little activity on the island and it was assumed that the small number of defenders present had been driven into the many tunnels. Ignoring the possibility of fire from heavy guns on the island, USN warships moved in close to provide fire support to the operation.

In spots 'Topside' was 500' above sea level and the jump would be at 600' AGL (Above Ground Level). Photos tell me the jumps were somewhat lower. Strong winds were expected, so the scatter-factor could be high. The landing zones were small and paratroops would face considerable danger of going into the cliffs or water. Gliders would probably have been a better choice to get down in such a small area, but there were none in the Pacific. So, after bombing and shelling from 23 January to 15 February 1945, on the 16th the 503's jump took place.

Fifty-one C-47s made the one hour flight north from a newly captured airfield on Mindoro Island.

Paradrops would be two 'lifts' of 1,000 men each. Jumps had to be exceptionally fast and tight to get into the small DZs. But little or no ground fire was anticipated.

Despite 35 knot winds coming from the north, the airlift and paratroops appear to have 'nailed' the DZs with nearly every chute on the old golf course. This photo looks southeast and shows that US Navy destroyers weren't hesitant about approaching the 'battery end' of Corregidor in defiance of the additional proximity of guns on Fort Hughes behind them (just beyond upper left).

Note wrecked buildings in the foreground proving Japanese neglect of the island since 1942.

Looking northeast from past Monja Battery (near water at center), the photo shows landings on the golf course (at right) with a few chutists trapped on the cliffs. Fewer men missed the drop zone in the landing between the parade ground and Battery Wheeler (on left). Surprise was achieved as planned, insuring the second lift and amphibious landings would be successful.

Some men reported firing at defenders on the way down. The Japanese fought back furiously but futilely. Parachute infantry quickly took control of high ground and batteries, eliminating Japanese troops on 'Topside' and the unlikely chance that one of the vintage guns might be put into action. As planned, the landing also drove Japanese into 'Middleside' caves (the slope between 'Topside' and 'Bottomside'), allowing easier beach landings of regular infantry on the only places landing craft could put ashore.

503rd RCT.

Looking roughly northeast across the north end of Corregidor. Battery Wheeler is on the left, Battery Crockett on the right. That is probably Mount Limay on Bataan Peninsula in the background. The golf course DZ is on the right and we see some of the parade ground DZ on the left. A drop is in progress over the golf course but the trailing aircraft seems too high. It may be on another mission.

At photo bottom is a USN patrol craft moving fast, probably there to rescue any paratroops landing short of the island.

Looking south, this photo shows road and rail lines climbing to the right toward 'Topside'. Amphibious landings took place on both north and south sides of 'Bottomside' (to the left). Numerous landing and support craft, and at least one cruiser have moved close-in to the island, ignoring a possible Japanese response from Fort Mills. Land in the distance (top of photo) is the south coast of the entrance to Manila Bay. US naval vessels were apparently not intimidated by Japanese still occupying the guns of Fort Drum.

Despite many more defenders on Corregidor than anticipated and a strong Banzai charge by 500 Japanese Marines near Battery Smith (the extreme west end of the island), US troops quickly gained and maintained control of the island. The most important Manila Bay Fort was in US hands by 21 February.[16] Mopping up took another five days, during which many Japanese who refused to surrender were sealed in tunnels and blown up (or blew themselves up). Only 19 defenders survived. The 503rd lost 169 KIA and 531 wounded (plus some 280 injured in the drop itself). Losses for 34th Infantry Regiment were 38 KIA and 153 wounded.

The fall of Corregidor set in motion the liberation of Manila and opening Manila Bay to Allied shipping. That led to quickly surging troops north on Luzon. Some fighting continued until August.

---

16. Honoring their achievement, the 503rd Parachute Infantry Regiment adopted 'The Rock' for their unit nickname.

On 2 March 1945, General MacArthur erased the most nettling stain on his record, presiding as victorious infantry and paratroops assembled on the Parade Ground before the old barracks to raise the Stars and Stripes. Note: chutes still draped in the trees of the DZ. MacArthur is in khakis in front of the lower formation, right under the flag (US Army photo).

The flag pole was a cast iron sectional mast taken from a Spanish warship surrendered after defeat by Admiral Dewey in May 1898. It had flown an American Flag for five decades. To a man steeped in tradition, General MacArthur was sensitive to its meaning—to his men and to the people of the Philippines.

I remember as a child hearing the emotion in the general's impressive voice over the radio as he said, 'I see that the flagpole still stands. Have your troops hoist the colors to its peak, and let no enemy ever haul them down.'

PACIFIC AIRLIFT

Allied and Axis troop carrier aircraft had been performing resupply services for engaged forces since early in the war. In Asia there were nuances of difference with European efforts in Tunisia and Russia because Allied troops in New Guinea and Burma were more scattered and often operating without a recognizable FEBA. Air resupply was generally a paradrop situation, frequently in nominally held enemy territory.

AIR COMMANDOS

In 1944 Project 9 created the US Army Air Corps' 1st Air Commandos with 13 C-47s and 100 CG-4A gliders to facilitate forward movement of British Major General Orde Wingate's Chindit army in Burma. Chindits were an irregular force comprised of elements of the 77th Indian Infantry Brigade, Black Watch, Kings Liverpool Regiment, 2nd Gurkha Rifles and 2nd Battalion Burma Rifles. They normally operated deep behind enemy lines and air resupply, mainly air drops, kept them viable. The Chindit mission was to keep Japanese pressure off General Stillwell's Chinese Divisions advancing west in Northern Burma.

A major initiative was planned for 5 March 1944. Air Commandos had their roots in German airlift/air-assaults in Spain, Norway and North Africa but unlike other Allied airborne operations, this one wasn't a combat assault, nor was it supporting Allies on a FEBA. Resupply and reinforcement missions deep into enemy territory was the Air Commando stock-in-trade, but this landing was different. Combat Engineers and their heavy equipment would be glider-landed to improve natural cleared areas deep in Burma, creating airfields 200 miles east of the Chindwin River, 70 miles SSW of Myitkyina.

The northernmost landing was 'Blackpool,' a position cutting Japanese road and rail lines running south from Myitkyina. That roadblock was held for 17 days against furious Japanese reaction.

Another of the three ad hoc landing sites selected ('Piccadilly') had been used earlier for C-47 landings to evacuate wounded and the enemy knew about it. Last minute photoreconnaissance showed the Japanese had strewn that field with large logs, making landing impossible.

So all gliders were sent to a previous unused location 20 miles farther north dubbed 'Broadway'.

An erroneous recall resulted in some of the force turning back to Imphal, Assam but 37 of the 54 double-towed gliders arrived at 'Broadway' (eight others landed in friendly territory west of the Chindwin).

'Broadway' had some logs strewn in the field and the surface had holes and ruts not apparent on aerial photos, so landing was rougher than expected. Nearly all the gliders were damaged but three bulldozers survived, allowing Engineers to quickly improve the landing ground into an airfield. Below is 'Broadway' after improvement. There were no repair facilities and all supplies, including drums of fuel, had to be flown in.

On 6 March, 62 more USAAF and RAF C-47 lifts brought in more men and equipment and over the next six days the strength had increased to thousands of men, dozens of ponies, 1000 mules and 500,000 lbs. of supplies. It was a week before the Japanese realized what was going on behind them.

Attacks on Japanese airfields began as P-51s and B-25s began to use 'Broadway' but the enemy couldn't be sure when Allied planes would be present. A strong air base far into Burmese 'no-man's-land' was devastating to the Japanese.

Japanese fighters and bombers tried many times to destroy the base and planes staging from it. Both sides took heavy losses but 'Broadway' remained in operation.

In April another similar mission was successful 200 miles behind Japanese lines, bringing in reinforcements and increasing the Chindit force in Burma to three brigades. First Air Commando kept Allied forces supplied with similar, if smaller, operations through the end of the war as the Japanese were methodically squeezed out of Burma. Capture of Myitkyina opened up road traffic over the mountains into China. Ledo Road saw its first convoy to China on 12 January 1945.[17]

17. In 1960 I served with Major William A. Glass who as a Lieutenant was in charge of a section on that first convoy. Ah, the stories he told….

Chapter IX

THE FINAL OPS

VARSITY

Since October 1942 Field Marshal Montgomery had worn a tanker's black beret bearing his rank badge and a Royal Tank Regiment cap badge. He relished his reputation as an armored leader. Since D-Day he'd longed to unleash his armored charges in open terrain for a race to Berlin. That was negated by decisions at Yalta in February when Allied leaders agreed Soviet forces would take the city. However, The North German Plain was 'natural tank country' and much of northern and western Germany could be secured by a rapid focused thrust similar to the German advance in western Belgium and France in 1940. To reach terrain where armored fire and maneuver would rule the field, Montgomery had to cross the Lower Rhine and get through or around the line of West Wall/Siegfried defenses. A thrust north over the Rhine was tried and failed at Arnhem, then delayed by the Battle of the Bulge. Several other plans died, overtaken by events.

Pre-war photo of the five-span steel truss cantilever road bridge at Wesel. This was one of the last German bridges over the Lower Rhine. Monty wanted to cross here.

On 7 March US First Army units 65 miles to the south of Wesel crossed the Rhine at Remagen on a railroad bridge the German Army had failed to destroy. Patton's Third Army was over the Rhine at Oppenheim near Frankfurt. Two hundred fifty miles east, the Wehrmacht was trying to hold a line on the Vistula and a Soviet Army was pressing in on Danzig. The German Army couldn't afford to give an inch along the Lower Rhine.

Wesel's rail and road bridges were both intact on recon imagery of 12 September 1944. British 21st Army Group dreamed of capturing them intact and flooding tanks toward Berlin. Sharp eyes will note 21 barrage balloons defending the road bridge.

On 10 March German Army units west of the northern Rhine crossed to the east and blew the remaining bridges. There would be no Remagen for Montgomery.

The German Army could tell a river crossing near Wesel was inevitable and dug in to make it expensive for the Allies. They expected an airborne component in the assault.

With the war clearly coming to a conclusion in Europe, a Rhine crossing at Wesel was laid on. Operation Plunder would use seventeen infantry divisions, eight armored divisions and two airborne divisions. Montgomery insisted on airborne unit support. The parachute and glider part of Plunder was Operation Varsity.

This time planning was careful and thorough, taking into account all the good and bad experiences of Normandy and Market Garden. An assault crossing of a large river had all the risks and hazards of the Normandy landings—vulnerable landing craft advancing against a determined, prepared defender in prepared positions. The Rhine was 350 yards wide north of Wesel and no one had illusions about crossing being a 'piece of cake'. With local German defenders augmented by units pulled back from east of the Rhine, forces around Wesel were now actually concentrated against just such a crossing. Particularly worrisome for the airborne component were the estimated 300 medium/light anti-aircraft guns and automatic weapons and gunners with plenty of experience against Allied aircraft. There were an estimated 8,000 enemy forces in the area north of Wesel. Ironically, one of the units facing Varsity landings was Germany's 1st Parachute Army.

Varsity was to land two airborne divisions just over the river to block reinforcements for defenders, eliminate artillery ranging on ground troops crossing the Rhine and take control of inland bridges needed for the advance. They would be an anvil for the onrushing hammer of infantry and armored divisions. All airborne LZs and DZs would be within four miles east of the Rhine, right on top of the most threatening defensive positions. The 6th AD mission was to take and hold Hamminkeln and bridges over the upper waters of the Issel (two miles east of the Rhine) to secure routes inland. They also had to clear defenders out of the forest between Hamminkeln and the Rhine and from high ground on the east bank.

British airborne units taking part were: 6th AD: 3rd Parachute Brigade, 1st Canadian Parachute Bn, 5th Parachute Bde, and 6th Airlanding Brigade. As usual for British airborne, the airlanding brigade had almost as many men as both parachute brigades combined. Many of those men had landing and combat experience in Normandy. Their DZ/LZs were farthest north with objectives near Hamminkeln and along the north end of the forest.

American 17th AD was comprised of 507th PIR, 513th PIR, and 194th Glider Infantry Rgt. Their mission was to take Diersfordter Wald and clear it of German artillery, then screen southeast toward Wesel. Some of those troops had fought as infantry in Belgium during the 'Bulge' but none had made a combat jump/landing. The new US 13th AD, training in England, was scrubbed from the plan because of inexperience and insufficient planes for the lift. Drop Zones for 17th AD were closer to Wesel and the road to Hamminkeln. 507th PIR was to land immediately south of Diersfordter forest (closer to Wesel).

Curtiss C-46 'Commando' troop carriers were to be used for the first time in Europe (they had been successfully flying the 'Hump' from India to China since 1944).

As seen here, there were jump doors on both sides of the fuselage.

A C-46 was about 50 knots faster than a C-47 and had a slower 'jump speed'. It could carry nearly double the number of paratroops in each load. Sticks of jumpers exited simultaneously from both sides of the fuselage for a tighter jump, as seen in this photo.

Those men are 'hooked up' and at least one has already exited from each side (see static lines trailing out the doors). This is probably a practice jump but the troopers are 'combat equipped' with weapons in protective bags and all the things needed for several days combat on the ground in their pouches and pockets. That large jump bag or 'leg bag' will be kicked out ahead of the jump and dangle ten to fifteen feet below him in descent so the trooper's legs don't have to support landing an extra 30 to 75 pounds. A British invention first tried in Normandy, the bags were notorious for tearing away if jump speed was too high.

Unfortunately, the C-46 had a serious flaw. C-47 'Dakotas' had all been equipped with self-sealing fuel tanks in their wings—the 'Commandos' had only been in theater for a month and had yet to be retrofitted with self-sealing fuel tanks. Flying low for jumps, ground fire puncturing a fuel cell would let gas and fumes fill spaces in the wing, creating a huge risk of fire. A sobering number of the planes were lost this way to ground fire during Varsity.

The loss of 19 out of 72 C-46s used caused Major General Matthew Ridgway, XVIII Airborne Corps Commander, to forbid using C-46s for future airborne operations.[18]

Varsity was also the only combat use of RAF C-54s as glider tugs (unverified by photos), and the only use of the Horsa Mk II.

---

18. With self-sealing fuel tanks C-46s were successfully used for parachute operations into the 1950s.

Fifty-six other troop carrier aircraft were also lost as were 16 bombers on resupply drops. Many more planes were seriously damaged by ground fire. Twenty-seven gliders crashed or were shot down. Three-fourths of the gliders were damaged landing, like the ones below.

The CG-4As below got down intact, but a Horsa in British livery wasn't as fortunate. The circle and marks on the photo at left annotate three individuals in the field near a Waco. Most likely this is an American LZ.

In another innovation, eight US serials, flying from Poix, France, double-towed CG-4As.[19] Dual tows were slower, making them even more vulnerable to ground fire. For safety, dual towline releases were 3,000 to 3,500 AGL. That made glider descents too long and slow, causing more losses to heavy AW fire. The British also released single gliders at 3,500 feet. Normal US glider release was 600 feet. Double-towing gliders proved to be a mixed blessing. It got more men over the target with fewer troop carrier aircraft, but if tow pilots were spooked by ground fire and jinked or changed altitude or speed, gliders could crash into each other or disintegrate from stress.

American parachute jumps were from 400-600' AGL resulting in well concentrated landings. The British jumped higher but were not excessively scattered because of it. Longer descent time did result in more paratroops being killed by ground fire as they descended, but resulted in less damage to tow planes.

Airborne personnel losses were also high in Varsity; greater than in the Normandy Invasion, with 819 KIA, 1,794 wounded and 580 missing, divided about evenly between 6th AD and 17th AD, but all objectives were secured by 1400 hours on 24 March 1945.

Allied ground forces moved up to the Rhine on 22 March and heavy bombing of the objective area began. Several days of an intense barrage from 3,500 artillery pieces began on 23 March, intended to take out much of the defense capability. Of course all that preparation completely eliminated the element of surprise. The 15th (Scottish) Infantry Division assault river crossing began during the night of 23 March, providing some modicum of surprise for airborne forces arriving thirteen hours later. The artillery barrage was lifted as Varsity aircraft crossed the Rhine the morning of 24 March.

A double-towing C-47 crosses the Rhine, inbound for a 194th Glider Infantry Regiment LZ south of Hamminkeln.

19. One C-47 towing two CG-4As had been successful in the China-Burma theatre but this was the first use in Europe.

Another view of a double-tow from inside a CG-4A.

Some Wacos brought in light anti-tank guns, Jeeps and supply trailers. Perhaps 'Garland Ray' was the pilot of the glider on the left? A Texan perhaps?

The 24 March 1945 series of aerial reconnaissance photos below were taken shortly before the airborne landings. They show the typical late winter haze that made ID of landing sites difficult for both troop carrier and glider pilots.

Wesel is at upper right. Both of the large bridges have dropped spans. The upper bridge (rail), completed in 1874 and destroyed on 10 March 1945, was 6,400 feet long (because of long approaches over the flood plain) and the last Lower Rhine river bridge blown by withdrawing German forces. Bomb and shell craters stipple the area.

The next photo is five miles north of Wesel. Hamminkeln is at upper right and the east edge of Diersfordter forest at lower left. The distance between the two is a little over a mile. Comparison with Google Maps that worked so well for Normandy and Market Garden images was extremely difficult since the area has changed so much since 1945—even many farm fields are significantly different. Hamminkeln was tiny compared to its present size and, from what I can see, the forest was actually smaller than it is today. Fortunately the rail line and some of the roads have kept the same alignment so locations can be identified.

So, where was all that advanced bombing and artillery barrage? Not here, six miles from the Rhine! There are fires in the woods at lower right but there is only one bomb/shell crater on the frame. The five exposures it took to cover from the Rhine just west of Wesel to Hamminkeln show bomb or shelling damage near the river and there are a few craters half way to Hamminkeln, most certainly bombing to interdict the rail line between Wesel and Emmerich. Of course, as we have seen, there was a lot of cratering on both sides of the Rhine at Wesel itself.

At first I thought those seven holes/pits just east of the forest were bomb craters, but comparison with an obvious bomb/shell crater in the field to the right, and their alignment, caused me to rethink. I now see them as possible weapons revetments between the forest and Hamminkeln. The arc on the upper four is typical of field artillery (not AAA guns which would have been in a circle). A curving line of holes like that is also uncharacteristic of bombing (and where is the bombing target?). I can't scale the enlargement properly but guess the revetments to be less than 30 feet in diameter. Since there are no openings in them to permit a heavy, towed gun to enter, I suggest they are for light artillery/automatic weapons. They are unoccupied and there are no tracks leading to them. Artillery within range of the Rhine crossings was a major target for Varsity airborne troops.

One way to load on a C-46 was to use the parallel vehicle ramps. These troops are flying as passengers, no helmets or weapons and not in jump gear.

Some of the 2,700 gliders being readied for the trip to Wesel. Tow cables are laid out on the tarmac and it looks like these are going to be double-tows.

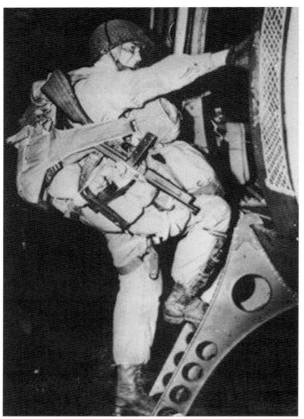

Airborne infantry loaded into troop carriers and gliders (British in England and Americans in France) for rendezvous near Brussels and a straight run to Wesel from the southwest.

Typical kit is seen on a fully 'Combat Equipped' 101AD jumper climbing into a C-47 for Overlord. On his back is a T-5 chute. A reserve chute is on his chest. Below it is a musette bag for personal items. Also on his belt are a first aid kit and canteen. Rations were in pockets on pant legs. He has a Thompson .45 caliber submachine gun and extra loaded magazines. A knife is strapped on his leg and he may have also carried a Colt 1911A1 .45 caliber automatic. A steel helmet with a parachute chin-strap completes requirements for a 'Combat Equipped Jump'. That gear weighed between 60–100 lbs. Quite a load for a man likely weighing between 150–180 lbs.

Some men needed a helpful push getting up the ladder into the plane with all that extra weight.

C-46s carried more jumpers on a single lift and two sticks could exit simultaneously. A higher door made a harder climb, so some men went up not yet in jump configuration. These troopers appear to have the new T-7 chute and reserve. They are armed with M-1 Garand rifles (in protective bags). Pockets in web-belts held spare loaded eight round clips. A trooper would have grenades in his jacket pockets. I don't see the knife, but they all carried at least one to cut shroud lines if necessary. The next trooper in line is wearing his chute but may sling it for the climb to get his reserve out of the way. We see the handle of his folding entrenching tool (shovel) showing behind his leg. By this time US paratroops had taken to wearing their first aid kit on the front of the helmet. The Mohawk haircut was a US airborne affectation begun for D-Day.

Leaving from 26 bases in England and France were 1,588 C-47s, 72 C-46s and 42 C-54s carrying 16,870 airborne troops and towing 1,320 Horsas and CG-4A/Hamilcars. Aircraft towing gliders took off first. Faster troop carriers with paratroops left later to 'time out' over the objective area together. Precision arrival of so many aircraft was an amazing feat of coordination. The stream of transport planes and gliders took two and a half hours to pass a single point and was shielded by more than 2,000 USAAF and RAF fighters.

This briefing is for troop carrier crews taking 194th GIR to LZ N south of Hamminkeln. Briefings like this were given at each launch base.

17th AD.

Sediment build-up behind groynes indicates the river is running from right to left, making these aircraft flying southwest on a line north of Hamminkeln. That suggests they are probably RAF having just jumped or dropped elements of 6th Airborne Division. When this photo was taken British infantry divisions were crossing the Rhine just off the lower right corner.

The 507th PIR jumping into DZ W near Flüren, three miles northwest of Wesel.

Haze caused 513th PIR heading for DZ X to be dropped in the wrong place (in LZ W amid 6th AD). With others still landing, these troopers of the 513th PIR immediately set up a defense perimeter in an orchard just south of Hamminkeln.

Unlike Market jumps, in Varsity both British and American paratroops dropped right into the heart of enemy defenses. Some units took heavy casualties just getting on the ground but their sudden arrival in large numbers soon overwhelmed defenders. Almost all the jumps and glider landings went pretty much as planned, getting down within two miles of assigned DZ/LZs and troops assembling in minimum time. An exception was 513th PIR which was taken too far north and jumped into a British DZ near Hamminkeln. The GIs combined forces with 6th AD men to quickly root out German artillery firing on the Rhine crossings. Those large caliber guns weren't a threat to airborne troops, but they were to ground forces marshalling on both sides of the Rhine and Engineers attempting to build temporary bridges so tanks could cross.

The 6th AD Airlanding Brigade had LZs east, northeast and south of Hamminkeln and made them all.

Slated to land together just south of the Diersfordter Wald, DZ W, 507th PIR actually came down in two adjacent locations but quickly formed up and went after German artillery in the forest, accomplishing their mission by early afternoon.

As usual, glider landings were troubled by the fleeting time a pilot with little actual flight experience had to identify his LZ after tow-line release. Glider pilots had been shown aerial photos of their landing grounds but the scale was too large to show much surrounding terrain. If the pilot didn't spot his designated site quickly, he was losing altitude fast and the scope of terrain he could see was shrinking. Pilot decisions were complicated by smoke and haze (some fires, some from Allied artillery shells, some possibly from German passive defense smoke generators). The only choice left was to follow other gliders in—and hope.

Many of the wallowing gliders took a pounding from German Light Flak and AW fire as they were towed east over AAA-defense belts near the Rhine and/or as they circled to land after towline release.

Objectives of 6th AD were all secured by 1100 hours and those of the 17th AD shortly after. About nightfall, airborne troops linked with ground forces expanding east over the Rhine. Success was materially enhanced because airborne troops landed together in strength and concentrated on their objectives rather than syphoning off strength to guard landing and resupply locations.

At 1300 hours 240 converted bombers (mostly B-24s) began streaming over the area, each dropping 2.5 tons of supplies in 22 bundles.

On 25 March an F-5 of 363rd Tactical Reconnaissance Group carried its two 24" focal length Split Vertical cameras in a north-to-south run over Hamminkeln. Time is about 1030 hours.

This frame shows the unfinished Autobahn 1000 yards east of Hamminkeln. The Issel River Bridge (arrow) was an objective for 1st Royal Ulster Rifles. There are at least two Horsa gliders close to the bridge.

The ground haze that bedeviled glider landings is evident.

The next frame covered Hamminkeln itself (upper right) and shows at least 50 Horsas and one Hamilcar on the ground south of the village. This is the 6th Airlanding Brigade in LZ P.
Defensive trenches and firing positions for German infantry are salted throughout the area.

The Autobahn under construction, about 3500 yards southeast of Hamminkeln. Photo center and center left were landing grounds for 194th Glider Infantry Regiment—LZ S. The site is roughly half way between Hamminkeln and Wesel. Diersfordter Wald is a mile to the left. There are 20+ CG-4A gliders on the ground in fields between the arrows.[20]

20. Appreciation to Pat Curran and Hans den Brok of Whitebeam Battlefield Research Forum for help in identifying Varsity LZ/DZs. Hans is also at www.airbornetroopcarrier.com

Another frame south of Hamminkeln in the 194th GIR landing area shows many gliders on the ground and scattered over quite a distance, making LZ S about two miles long and at least a half mile wide. The village of Blumenkamp is in the lower right corner.

For map orientation; converging toward Wesel (beyond lower right), the northern straight line is the Hamminkeln rail line. Diagonalling through the center of the photo is the Hamminkeln-Wesel road. Running across the lower image is the Wesel-Emmerich rail line.

Enlargement of the upper left corner of the previous photo shows five Horsa and 40 Waco gliders on the ground. It is one of the tightest landing groupings in the operation.

The preceding four aerial photos were all taken by the LSV camera (Left Split Vert) of the recon plane making a run over Hamminkeln to the river.

Let's look at the RSV photos from that same 25 March mission.

There is the unfinished Autobahn again about 1000 yards northeast of Hamminkeln. The rail bridge (upper arrow) and road bridge (lower arrow) over the Issel River were objectives for 2nd Oxford & Bucks.

The then miniscule village of Ringenberg is north of the road (at upper right). Hamminkeln is just south of this photo.

There has been some prior bombing in the area.

The 6th AD's 2nd Ox & Bucks duplicated their performance in Normandy. Enlargement shows
17 Horsas landed within 300 feet of the two Issel bridge objectives.
Those are bomb craters, not the result of artillery fire.

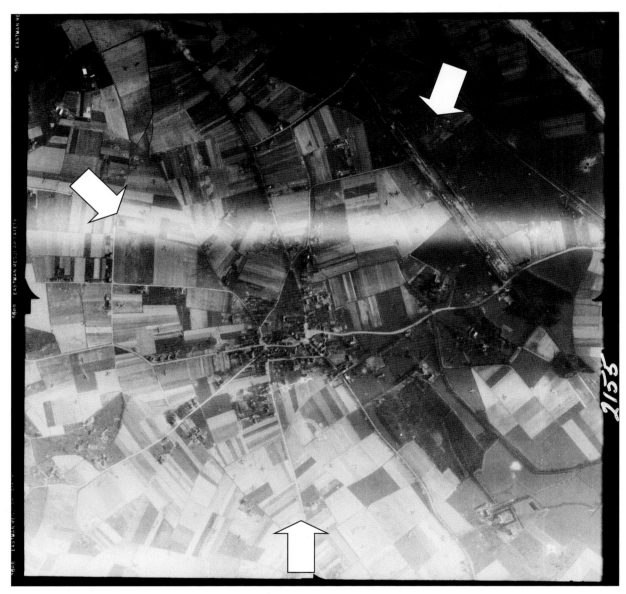

Hamminkeln is at photo center. There are 6th AD Airlanding Brigade gliders immediately above, to the left and south of the village, but no large, tight concentrations like Arnhem.

A few seconds south of Hamminkeln, this 'recce jock' saw something that caught his attention. It was to his right about a mile south of Hamminkeln. Like any good recce pilot, he cranked up a wing to let his RSV camera reach out to cover the activity.

What he imaged was more of the 194th GIR landing and possibly chutes of one of the 507th PIR drop zones (woods at left arrow and in with gliders at right arrow).

There are 100+ Wacos and Horsas on the ground.

Enlargement of the lower left of the previous photo shows gliders and some probable parachutes on the ground. This imagery is south of Hamminkeln on 25 March 1945.

Wings level and back on course again; the recce mission covered the main landing zone for 194th GIR, north of Wesel (LZ S). I count 200 gliders on this frame. Most gliders are in a 500 foot-wide band between the two arrows.

There are also a few possible chutes. I was surprised to see only a few parachutes in this series of imagery though it covers almost the entire landing area from north of Hamminkeln to Blumenkamp.

Enlargement between the arrows on the preceding photo shows Horsa and Waco landings were from west to east. These glider pilots found good, flat, open fields but the landings are not as tight as some in Market Garden.

Probably the 507th PIR drop northwest of Wesel. Dark chutes (tan or OD) are jumpers. White chutes were for supplies, to make them easier to locate on the ground.

These enlargements are another look at the 194th Glider Infantry Regiment landing southeast of Hamminkeln. There are 100 gliders on the ground on this image, most of them CG-4As. Good choice of fields made for good landings.

Enlargement of the center of the previous image.

Within two days there were a dozen light bridges over the Rhine and 14 Allied Divisions were pouring east in Germany north of Wesel. By early April US Engineers had a more substantial bridge built on piers of the old Wesel rail bridge. Operation Varsity had achieved its goals and established a record that still stands as the largest single airborne assault on a single place in a single day. It was a fitting way to close out airborne operations in Europe.

ONCE MORE UNTO THE BREECH?
Euphoria over the success of Varsity had engineers reclaiming Varsity gliders for reuse and HQ planners continuing work on Operation Eclipse, landing 17th AD, 82nd AD and a brigade of British 6th AD near Berlin. Perhaps someone realized the operation would probably lose most of the force and thoroughly infuriate the Soviets, who viewed Berlin as their prize. Thankfully General Eisenhower cancelled that operation on 28 March 1945.

Swift ground advances after Varsity and Soviet troops nearing Berlin led to a crumbling of the German Army. The Battle for Berlin began on 20 April, Hitler shot himself on 30 April and Germany surrendered on 7 May 1945.

LAST ONE TURN OFF THE MUSIC
The final airborne operation of the Second World War occurred on 23 June 1945. Six CG-4As and one CG-13[21] were used in a glider assault to capture Camalaniugan Airfield on the north coast of Luzon in the Philippines. There was little Japanese resistance and the mission was quickly accomplished.

---

21. An upgraded version of the Waco able to carry 30 to 40 troops. As far as I know this was its only combat use. CG-13s were used to carry supplies in France and England.

Chapter X

AFTERTHOUGHTS

It turned out most large airborne operations were effective but not the hoped for magic bullet to dominate any field and decide any battle—though they came close several times.

Mistakes and advantages in airborne ops weren't always clear right after a major landing, but the time it took to bring airborne units back up to strength and readiness usually allowed for the worst aspects of prior planning to be understood and avoided. Tactics such as concentrated troop carrier strength and timing (TOT—Time Over Target) were better appreciated but not easier to achieve, as were the best ways to reinforce and effectively resupply with gliders and para-drops. The very essence of an airborne operation was a sudden rush of highly focused force. Resupply air-drops from converted heavy bombers were found to be very successful. Those planes could carry more than C-47s and were faster in and out of ground fire zones.

As the war progressed, most airborne operations stood on the shoulders of preceding operations, copying what worked, learning from the mistakes, gradually evolving a smooth functioning, well-coordinated, nearly irresistible force. But experience also showed airborne troops had to have reasonable objectives that contributed to an overall op.

The most important factors for a successful airborne operation were keeping objectives within reach and focusing airborne troop strength on them. When properly used, the surprise insertion of elite light infantry behind (or in the midst of) enemy positions proved decisive, but increasing mobility of ground forces and proliferation of high rate-of-fire automatic weapons made that advantage short lived. Airborne lodgments had to be followed by rapid linkage with more heavily armed ground forces. Isolated light infantry holding out for nine days at Arnhem was unprecedented. So were times when ground-delivered airborne units stood their ground for long periods fighting as part of a regular larger force.

It was also important to get airborne troops onto the ground without excessive loss of men and equipment to ground fire during the run-in. Landing accidents and techniques were steadily refined. As war began, German forces led the way and all their landings were in daylight. The Allies looked at German losses and tried night landings when actually the answer was lower AGL jumps. But not too low—the canopy had to fully deploy.

Night landings were safer from ground opposition but higher in landing casualties and bad for unit assembly on the ground. Defensive weapons and tactics always adjust to new concepts, making glider and parachute landings more vulnerable as defenders learned how to combat them. By the end of the Second World War the Allies, the only ones still in the game, were back to single-lift daylight landings. Assault landings by transports fell out in 1941.

The two biggest problems that were never solved were (1) poor unit-to-unit/unit-to-air radio communications and, (2) difficulties tow and glider pilots had identifying DZ/LZs in time to hit them accurately.

Assessing the success of airborne operations, we must also remember that bold initiatives such as Norway, Holland, Crete, D-Day, Market Garden and Varsity wouldn't have been possible if friendly fighter planes hadn't had absolute control of the air overhead.

German interest in airborne operations blossomed from 1938 to 1942 because it fit well with offense—Blitzkrieg warfare—narrow objectives taken in a rush, opening doors for fast-moving Panzers. Germany already had a thriving glider community and they watched the Soviets developing parachute landing techniques. When they went to war in the east, broad expanses and broad objectives were better suited to sweeping armored thrusts than the necessarily leapfrogging point focus of airborne assault. German airborne strength suffered high losses from unanticipated ground resistance in several operations—a lesson the Allies would re-learn in Sicily in 1943. From 1943 on, the Germans were on defense and airborne is not a good defense tool.

Impressed by German successes in 1940, but before lessons learned could be digested, airborne units began organizing in Britain in 1941. Parachute skills were almost immediately used, mainly for introducing agents in German-held Europe and for small unit special missions like the Bruneval Raid in 1942. Formation and use of larger units had to wait for 1943 and offensive opportunities in the Mediterranean. By that time the Americans had caught up. British and US airborne capabilities quickly grew to regimental and then division-size.

The following observations and conclusions are mainly based upon what I saw on imagery as I wrote this book, and what I learned during 27 years of active service in military Intelligence. None of my comments should be taken as criticism of what men did in combat. The old military saying 'All the Brothers are Valiant' was largely true for airborne. It took stones to jump or airland into combat behind enemy lines—still does. Troops go where they're told and do what they have to do; however there is no reason to be shy about being skeptical of the motives and abilities of some of the decision-makers, planners and leaders involved. Nor can troop carrier aircrew performance escape a hard look.

It is impossible to work on something like this without forming opinions and I'll admit I may not fully understand all I know, so, I'll just call 'em like I see 'em as we take a critical look back at the operations just covered. Remember, the focus is on the airborne op; the where, why and how troops were put on the ground and how they met their initial tasking, not subsequent ground actions.

Let's get three things out of the way right off. After writing this book, what do I think was the best airborne division of the Second World War?

I wouldn't touch that one with a 10 foot pole (even if it was someone else's pole). All the Airborne divisions, regiments and battalions—German, British, American, Japanese and Soviet—were fiercely courageous and steadfast to their duty. In a word, magnificent light infantry. However, not all were well employed. If I had to pick a unit, I'd lean toward the 82nd Airborne Division's 505th Parachute Infantry Regiment because of the many different jumps and battles it survived without defeat. A close second would be 504th PIR. Some German units also had long and illustrious records in combat—but not with the jump/landing component being involved.

What do I believe was the best airborne operation in the Second World War?

No question on this one. The Blue Ribbon goes to Britain's 6th Airborne Division landing on D-Day. Excellent planning kept objectives simple and attainable (two point targets and two blocking missions) and the Division's successes contributed directly to the overall Overlord mission. Four landing sites[22] kept the force concentrated and near targets so they could be taken quickly and held. Drops and glider landings were on target and tight. Surprise was achieved and all initial tasks completed before first light on 6 June 1944. You can't do better than that.

The Grandfather of all Second World War glider landings, the brilliant German landing atop Fort Eben Emael is second only because it was miniscule in comparison.

Two large Soviet drops vie for worst airborne operation of the war.

---

22. Six if you count the small LZs just north and south of Pegasus Bridge.

It must be remembered that airborne infantry was, after all, infantry that rode to work in a plane or glider. That ride was controlled by someone else who, hopefully, set them down in the right place. Except for being behind enemy lines, once on the ground they might just as well have been delivered by a truck or landing craft. Indeed, US 82nd and 101st AD won undying fame and honor without an airlift when they were trucked in to stop German advances in Belgium during the Battle of the Bulge. The same was true of Fallschirmtruppen on the ground at Cassino, Italy, the Eastern Front and in France.

Clearly it wasn't the skill of an air component that made airborne forces special. Floating to earth in a chute or glider didn't kill enemy or take ground. It was the will and determination of elites once on the ground that made them special. When a unit goes into battle there is always a question. Will they stand? Will they fight? With an airborne infantry unit that question was already answered. The guts it took to ride wings into battle and the winnowing of their rigorous training made those men tough, determined—and proud. Too proud to bend or break. There was no 'quit' in them. What they had to do to earn jump wings had already taken them beyond that point. Regardless of nationality—it was the same. Commanders knew those were men who'd been tested, men who could be counted upon, men who must be respected and feared in battle.

But this is a book about airborne operations, so let's look at the major events critically. The first rule was to put the fighting force down as a unit and in the right place to accomplish their mission.

Air assault on Norway was rudimentary; a redux of something the Germans had done successfully in Spain. The airlift landings were unopposed and couldn't have been done anywhere a year later in the war. Luftwaffe had plenty of transports and fighters, and it was a long haul to Norway for British air and naval intervention. The operation was well planned and adequately manned. Troops were put where they could achieve most. Disgorging from transports, they quickly took key airfields, allowing landing of other infantry to assault other objectives. Once airfields were taken and German fighters landed, the game was over. The op was successful because opponents were taken by surprise and overwhelmed—establishing the Airborne Standard. Potential opposing forces (Norwegian and British) weren't ready and/or were based too far away to react in time. However, a lesson should have been learned from the high rate of transport aircraft lost despite only light ground fire.

Invasion of Belgium and Netherlands opened with the masterful Eben Emael assault. The op was ideal for airborne capability of the day. The attack was small in scope and limited to a single key objective that was important to a larger operation. Use of gliders was genius. Surprise was complete because German planes didn't overfly the target to alert it (surely the 1944 taking of Pegasus Bridge in Normandy was a direct descendant of Eben Emael). Small unit simultaneous paradrops to take key Dutch bridges were rudimentary but equally successful, mainly because of light opposition. Larger airlift and airborne attacks, particularly against Rotterdam, incurred high losses, again revealing the vulnerability of transport aircraft used to land troops. It took heavy Luftwaffe bombing to punish Rotterdam and shock it into surrender— a lesson London refused to learn a few months later.

Different American and British philosophies of airborne assault were shaped by Eben Emael and the German advance on Rotterdam. The British started first and viewed jumpers as small units to take control of a landing ground, clearing it so large numbers of infantry, field guns and vehicles could be swiftly inserted using gliders. That let them go in initially a little heavier in armament. A Horsa lifted 25 airlanding infantry. The load was together and immediately assembled with other nearby glider lifts to quickly form platoons, companies and battalions. It worked for them because they had a good-sized, versatile glider. American units were formed a little later and preferred parachute infantry jumping in large numbers to maximize surprise and concentration of force, with gliders bringing in reinforcements, equipment and supplies when LZs were secured. A C-47 carried 28 paratroops, but jumpers went out in 'sticks' that could string them out over as much as a mile; more with cross winds or a higher AGL jump.

Corinth Canal and Crete ops were forced on the Germans by an offensive they didn't originally intend and had to end quickly because of the impending Invasion of the Soviet Union. Without typical German meticulous planning, neither operation went well. Objectives on Crete were too obvious, too many and too scattered for mutual support; plus there was little hope of rapid relief by surface forces. A Pyrrhic victory on Crete resulted with more high loss rates for Ju 52s occurring just before they were badly needed for Operation Barbarossa. Unexpectedly intense ground opposition on landing and afterward all but destroyed the German airborne division. Personnel and equipment losses were never fully made up, so Crete marked the end of German airborne offensives. Elite German airborne formations fought as regular infantry for the remainder of the war.

Nadzab was a well-conceived and well-planned regimental-sized parachute Op. Near perfect operationally, cleanly achieving the initial objective (a forward airfield) without ground opposition. It had a flavor of 'overkill,' designed with no possibility of failure, but it didn't result in eliminating the enemy force it outflanked. An essential element of a good airborne operation is RISK—pushing the capability to the limit to get maximum result.

Allied forays into larger airborne offensives in Sicily and southern France supporting large onshore landings were poorly planned and not well matched to the overall operation or the terrain. It appeared airborne capability wasn't really understood and units were used as ad hoc scouts/skirmishers: largely side shows. Perhaps that's how the old guard 'leg infantry' brass thought of them. Nearly everything that could go wrong did, and the post-op learning-curve was steep. Losses came from 'friendly fire' off shore, landing in rough terrain and intense ad hoc ground opposition. Objectives were taken but with near prohibitive costs. Regular infantry were experiencing the same wastage as Allied commanders struggled to learn new rules for combat.

Operation Overlord showed airborne assault had come of age—and what it could do. The British 6th AD contribution is discussed above. Surprise and dawn H-Hours for beach landings dictated airborne forces had to go in just after midnight. The two American airborne divisions were added to the mix late in the game and had less time for planning and selecting DZs. They also had more difficult navigation and landing conditions than 6th AD, having to find many widely scattered, hard to identify Drop Zones and objectives which divided their force into 'penny packets'. More scattering of the force came when drop zones were not hit well (often many miles from the right place). The plan was too complex so too much could go wrong, and some of the units had no combat experience. A 101st AD trooper fell on his way to the door of a C-47. By the time he was on his feet and jumped with the rest of his stick they were miles from their DZ and virtually out of play. On D-Day, the 'Airborne Spirit' prevailed everywhere and troopers in bad drops rose to the occasion, eventually achieving all assigned objectives or just ranging in the night, raising hell with the confused Germans. However, if 4th Infantry Division hadn't done so well getting off Utah Beach, American airborne forces farther inland would have had a much rougher two days after landing.

I see the much-maligned Market Garden as airborne assault fully matured. Normandy lessons learned; the drops and landings would be in daylight for more precision. For the first time airborne would land perpendicular to the FEBA rather than parallel to it. The bold concept involving three airborne divisions raised airborne ops from a supporting role to leading the campaign. Blunting the V-2 assault on England and getting a powerful armored force over the Rhine into northern Germany were sound strategic objectives, and key bridges ahead of advancing armor were valid tactical objectives. Despite criticism of the op, airborne units took every objective but one (Nijmegen Bridge) on the first day and held them for a reasonable time. If XXX Corps had reached the Lower Rhine two days earlier and pushed on another mile, Market Garden would be studied today in every War College as a brilliant coup. Those two needed days almost exactly match time lost crossing the Waal at Nijmegen. Unfortunately, close only counts in horseshoes, curling and hand grenades.

POOR/HASTY PLANNING RESULTED IN THREE WEAKNESSES

First: XXX Corps should have provided for a parallel/alternate line of advance to compensate where strong defense or destroyed bridges delayed an attack axis. Rail lines and bridges to the west (particularly from Maas to Waal) could easily accommodate tanks but were not used. There was apparently insufficient strength to frequently pass fresh armored units through battered, exhausted units to the lead. Good planning always expects, and tries to provide for, losses and things going wrong. I know battles are fought with what commanders have and know (or think they know) and the situational pressures they are under, but surely a commander with Montgomery's experience understood things would go wrong and delays could occur, particularly after his own failure three months earlier to advance eight miles inland and make his 6 June objective of Caen.

Market Garden was out of character for Montgomery (unless you believe his motive was to place himself at the head of the Allied Army ending the war). He had a history of building up a mountain of troops and material then pushing it over on the enemy, moving forward a few miles and building a new pile. Surely he and his staff were aware that a rushing ground advance against reluctantly withdrawing German forces could expect delays and surprises. Even so, he postulated a Rommel-like one-tank-wide dash of 60 miles beyond the FEBA, with little protection for the flanks, and no timing slack for anything going wrong. I'm surprised General Eisenhower approved a plan that so disrupted his Broad-Front Strategy. Perhaps the German V-2 barrage on England did trump all other considerations.

Second: 1st AD landing at Arnhem was understrength because of a shortage of tow-planes (an Airborne Corps Commander and staff with more combat experience would have helped too). After three decades of studying aerial photos of Arnhem I can't help wondering what might have happened if British 1st Airborne Division drop had been delayed one or two days and executed in a single lift using C-47s recycled from 82nd and 101st drops.[23] The complete 1st Airborne Division plus the Poles could have been landed in one lift. Of course some surprise might have been lost, but German reaction to the US drops the day(s) before would logically have been to rush available reserves south to meet the Allied drive (as did 9th SS Panzer's Reconnaissance Battalion in response to 82nd AD landings at Nijmegen on the 17th). Drawing defenders south from Arnhem would have given 1st Airborne the additional advantage of cutting off German defenders between the Rhine and Waal, forcing them to fight in two directions without logistical and communications support except from due east.

Another, perhaps more significant, option would have been to abandon 1st AD LZs on the 18th and concentrate the entire force at or near the bridge. That would, of course, have required the second (and third) lifts to come down somewhere else such as south of the river. Considering how long Frost and his handful of men held the buildings beside the bridge, how long might even half of the Division have held a larger part of the city if they'd moved in before the Germans could react? In urban warfare defense has the advantage. They might also have created an urban perimeter large enough for air-drop of supplies.

Third: making the situation worse, LZ selection at Arnhem violated lessons learned from Eben Emael, Nadzab and Pegasus Bridge as well as two basic principles of war: surprise and concentration of force. The well-known 'Bridge too Far' at Arnhem, wasn't necessarily too far north of Nijmegen, assuming the ground thrust progressed well. However, Arnhem Bridge was

---

23. Weather precluded the original plan to lift the three airborne divisions on three consecutive days. Landing 101st, 82nd then 1st AD sequentially might have been better than the way the plan unfolded.

5.5 miles from the 1st AD parachute DZ and 6.5 miles from glider LZs (that's just 2.5 miles less than the total distance south to Nijmegen). DZ Y was worse; 10 miles from mission objectives. British troops holding the Arnhem Bridge had a perilously long, easily interdicted 'life line' for supplies, ammunition and reinforcements and troops protecting the LZs were irrelevant to the bridge. Was LZ selection an excess of planning caution or inexperience of 1st Airborne Division brass? It seems as though 1st AD staff simply ignored 6th AD experience and success in Normandy (pig-headed or jealous?).

Squabbling between American, British and Polish airborne leaders didn't help the Op. Dueling generals is one thing, but why boldly go farther behind enemy lines than any prior airborne operation in history, then not be bold in selecting landing locations?

Apparently other potential landing sites north and south of Arnhem were rejected based upon RAF objections, because of flak units at Deelen Airdrome, five miles north of Arnhem. Those guns played no role against gliders or tugs staying near the Rhine.

The Arnhem force should have landed in open fields north and south of the Rhine closer to the Arnhem Bridge and moved their entire strength to Arnhem Bridge before defenders could react. Oh, I know the rationalizations: German AAA guns, soft ground, etc. I just don't buy them as valid. Ground fire for subsequent lifts was from automatic weapons moved south into range after the initial landings—not from Deelen AAA. The south bank is where Polish 1st Independent Parachute Brigade successfully landed on 22 September.

I've already shown where 82nd AD should have landed at least a company north of the river at Nijmegen, noted the four day delay for 82nd AD to take the Waal Bridge and XXX Corps' 19 hour delay at Nijmegen before pushing on north toward Arnhem.

Using 12 September 1944 imagery, I have annotated four large open areas at Arnhem that would have been my choices for LZs to put the bulk of 1st Airborne Division within rushing distance (less than two miles) of the objective before German forces could react. It would also have resulted in the same troops defending the LZs directly supporting those holding the bridge.

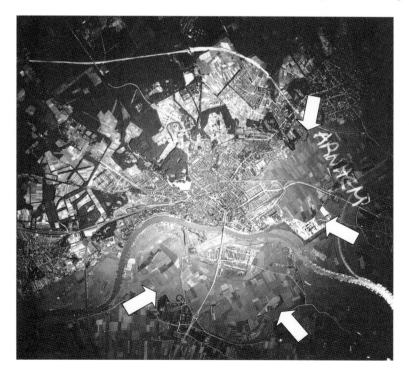

Landing south of the Rhine would have made the river a de facto protective barrier against the two German Armored Divisions. Some writers attribute the loss at Arnhem to those two Panzer divisions that happened to be recovering at Arnhem. Both were seriously under strength in men and equipment after Normandy. The initial opposition to 1st AD wasn't tanks, assault guns and self-propelled armored artillery. It was mainly Panzergrenadiers (heavy infantry). Admittedly they had mortars and artillery out-gunning the airborne troops, but it wasn't a case of heavy tracked vehicles crushing a path to the bridge over light infantry (German tanks and self-propelled artillery didn't have an impact for several days).

Frost and his men held their ground for four days and the rest of the Division, trapped in Oosterbeek and being squeezed against the river, held out for nine. What might have been done if even one more parachute battalion had immediately gone east to the bridge with Frost?

This pre-war photo from Intelligence Files shows Arnhem's narrow, winding streets closely flanked by densely sited multi-story buildings roughly 2,000 feet northwest of the target bridge. The Rhine is to the left. This is the area British reinforcements would have to transit or defend to support men at the bridge. That is defensive territory, decidedly unfriendly to armor. Urban density limits AFV maneuver and provides endless opportunity for defensive positions. Bends in roads shorten the effective range of large guns and men in upper floors have vantage points to attack tanks and assault guns from above and the rear.

What might have been done defending this urban terrain if Frost and his men had been kept supplied with ammunition and PIAT bombs?

A-6M3-HOLLAND-ARNHEM-N5158 E0555-RESTRICTED
1683.633

With concentration of force, a larger perimeter might have held the bridge until XXX Corps tanks could cross and push north of the Lower Rhine. A larger, well identified perimeter backing on the river would likely have made air resupply more successful (many supplies to Oosterbeek were dropped too high and fell outside British lines or into the river). The real impact of those German Armored Divisions occurred after the delay at Nijmegen allowed 10th Panzer (the slower to react) to assemble forces and move west to defend the route north to Arnhem, resulting in slower progress by XXX Corps.

Troop Carrier Command drops of American parachutists in Market Garden have been criticized by some authors, but most drops were on or near their targets. True, a few inexperienced transport crews panicked during heavy ground fire and made jumps too high or (tragically) too low, or at too high an airspeed (but not as many as in Overlord). Insufficient training of transport crews was a legitimate problem for Market. The 315th Troop Carrier Group analysis of Market said, 'The time element was too short for the proper collection of sufficient photographic coverage. Photomosaics of the DZ and LZ areas were provided, but they were of high altitude and not provided in sufficient quantities.' Hard to judge if that is a reason or an excuse.

From what I see, the north end of Market Garden failed because of poor planning and decisions. Arnhem Bridge was lost by a split-lift, then using most of the available force defending an LZ too distant to support the troops holding the bridge. The Nijmegen-Arnhem leg was lost by delays reaching, taking and crossing the Waal at Nijmegen then pushing north. Had the planned schedule been kept, crossing the Rhine would have still been problematic but possible.

Both 1945 airborne operations had a familiar feel—do it because we can. I saw enough of 'Everyone wants a piece of the action' from higher-ups during tours in Southeast Asia and years in Washington to recognize the scent.

Naturally no commander with troops in action and struggling will keep elite infantry sitting on their hands, but the war was clearly ending in both theatres and it looks like Army commanders, and probably the airborne units themselves, wanted one more combat jump. While heroic, vigorously fought and successful, in my opinion neither 1945 airborne initiative was strictly operationally necessary. Both probably helped shorten the war, but omission of either wouldn't have changed the outcome of the Second World War.

Like Nadzab, retaking Corregidor was designed with no possibility of failure. Accepting the operational objectives as valid, the op was classic airborne doctrine; surprise and overwhelm defenders. The island jump was bold considering the small size of the landing areas available. Putting almost all of 503rd Regimental Combat Team into two DZs each about 500 feet in diameter and flanked by cliffs ranks as the best single parachute delivery/landing of the war.

There would have been more landing casualties if the drops hadn't been virtually unopposed by ground fire, allowing a very low AGL jump. Parachute infantry did an excellent job of accomplishing what they were asked to do. The question is WHY do it? Were Japanese forces on 'the Rock' a threat? To whom? How? Were they firing at Allied shipping? Could they have? If that many troops (dropped and landed from boats) were needed, wouldn't it have resulted in fewer casualties to land them all from the sea?

Given progress in the Philippines, opportunities to use an elite unit like the 503rd were narrowing. More importantly, General MacArthur wanted Corregidor, and taking it with a big PR 'splash' would let everyone know he took it back (like Nadzab, his staff made sure there were plenty of photos). In fairness, MacArthur also understood the powerful emotional impact in the Philippines of retaking 'The Rock' but there is a distinct 'show boat' flavor to the operation.

Varsity is another operation requiring a hard look, considering the status of the war at that time and post-war criticism. That airborne op was a forward evolution in organization but a step backward in concept, reverting to employment closer to Overlord. Targeting Issel River bridges to prevent their destruction was classic airborne doctrine, but for the first time specific enemy defenses (artillery) threatening the advance were also targets.

In execution, Varsity certainly reflected the lessons of all earlier operations. It was well planned and put together but it put airborne in very much a supporting role without much risk, surrendering one of airborne assault's greatest assets. Airborne troops didn't even go in until well after the ground assault/river crossing had begun.

Overwhelming force was inserted in a single lift at a cautious distance beyond the FEBA—all landings within two-to-six miles beyond the Rhine and advancing heavy infantry and armor. Execution showed the lessons of earlier ops had been learned well. Jumping deeper beyond the FEBA where defenses were thinner might have resulted in fewer casualties...but targets are where they are. Daylight landings were in carefully chosen locations close to designated, easily identified, objectives. But Varsity again demonstrated that getting all jumpers and gliders precisely into specific, pre-selected locations was a planner's fantasy. Once again, credit for success goes to the airborne infantry because they quickly completed assigned missions regardless of landing means or location. Varsity was a success because of overwhelming force inserted in a small area against depleted and battered enemy forces with no air support—and knowledge on both sides that the war couldn't last much longer.

Allied planners and 'brass' knew the war was nearing conclusion but they were painfully aware that an overconfident mind-set resulted in being caught off guard in Belgium in December. Might the Wehrmacht pull another rabbit out of their helmet? No one wanted to find out, so Plunder/Varsity was important to keep the German Army off balance and retreating. The Germans couldn't defend everywhere, and Varsity showed Allied airborne forces might be landed anywhere.

Overlord lessons learned kept Varsity objectives limited and close together. Varsity also avoided the most serious mistake of Market Garden by selecting LZ/DZs near objectives. Relieving powerful ground forces just four miles away meant it wasn't necessary to bleed off airborne strength to defend landing sites—keeping troops focused on mission objectives. The entire operation was planned to be achievable in a short time.

Like Eben Emael, Pegasus Bridge and Grave Bridge, both paratroops and airlanding infantry got down quickly in the heart of enemy positions and did what they had to do in a rush. Setting records, Varsity was a fitting operation to end the airborne landings in Europe.

Some critics have opined that the elite light infantry could have done more with fewer casualties crossing the Rhine in boats. That would have wasted the huge psychological impact of a sudden hammer blow from the sky behind defenders. I deem Varsity overall a good operation because of the implied threat to German decision makers—they knew there were four more uncommitted Allied airborne divisions in England, and Varsity showed they might be used anywhere at any time.[24]

Varsity ensured Plunder (Rhine Crossing) would come off smoothly, resulting in rapid ground advances east. If Plunder/Varsity hadn't gone well, the Red Army might have been met somewhere west of the Elbe. West Germany (and perhaps modern Germany) would have been quite different. The impact of that on the Cold War can only be guessed.

The Second World War's final airlanding in the Philippines was almost a training exercise.

Given that troop proficiency was relatively constant except where refined by actual combat experience, the evolution of airborne operations, the increasing sophistication, was attributable to improved command (not always in evidence), more competent staff skills, better planning and organization—AND better integration of the unique properties of airborne assault in major ground offensives.

---

24. The Germans had no way of knowing the current readiness status of British 1st AD and American 13th, 82nd and 101st ADs. Allied deception schemes had troops in England being obvious in pubs and streets wearing shoulder patches of non-existent US airborne divisions.

Airborne Operations evolved to larger and more complex missions as commanders acquired understanding of what was possible and more confidence that missions could be accomplished.

The essence of an airborne op was like a knight's move in chess—a sudden jump to a non-contiguous location. Looking at all aspects of airborne assault objectively, I came to conclude that the real common denominator of first day airborne landing success was the courage and skill of airlift pilots plus the capacity and numbers of aircraft involved. Getting the force on the ground quick, clean, together and in the right place made a big difference. It was also important to size the force to the task. Eben Emael and Pegasus Bridge were perfect in size and execution, with a few gliders landing the small forces needed. Crete was a disaster because airlift couldn't get enough troops on the ground fast enough. Aircraft shortfall meant Arnhem Bridge had insufficient strength on the first landing. Varsity flooded the small objective area with troops.

Japan and the Soviet Union fell out of the game because losses didn't balance gains. Neither had the right planes or enough of them to swiftly introduce large, concentrated forces. The Germans had a marginally adequate transport but never enough of them, and the Ju 52s were too slow. Too many Ju 52s were lost in Norway, Netherlands and Crete for German industry to keep the Luftwaffe equipped to satisfy all competing requirements. After 1943 the transports were too desperately needed for supply missions in Russia and to North Africa to permit other use.

For most of the war the American C-47 was the best plane (best load and best speed) available for airborne work. Skytrain/Dakota aircraft were shared with the British who had a great glider (Horsa) they shared with US airborne divisions. More important, by 1944 there were plenty of both for Overlord. Three months later Market Garden was more ambitious and faltered in part for want of sufficient airlift capacity. Varsity finally put the whole package together. The flawed C-46 showed that higher capacity airlift was advantageous, landing more jumpers closer together.

More powerful air-transportable weapons were constantly improving throughout the war but airborne forces were still light infantry, ill-suited to stand long against heavy infantry and armor. That they did in Belgium in December 1944 is still a testimonial to the Airborne Spirit.

The only serious unresolved weak spots in airborne ops evolution were better ways to identify designated drop/landing locations from the air and more reliable, longer range communications—which are two sides of the same coin. Those problems awaited invention of the transistor in 1947.

WHAT NEXT

A C-130 carries 64 combat-equipped paratroops and a modern C-17 can carry 102 at 450 knots, but anti-aircraft weapons improvements have made it frighteningly easy to shoot down a transport plane. Today IMINT, ELINT and SIGNIT make it impossible to hide an airborne armada marshalling or in the air. Ten thousand men floating to earth in a night sky behind enemy lines is now in the same category with a thousand-plane bombing raid or the majestic passing of a line of post-Dreadnought battleships at Hampton Roads or Portsmouth. Awesome, but I doubt we'll see them again. Gliders are gone, and use of transport airlift for an assault didn't see the end of the war (revived briefly for a few Special Forces landings in Vietnam and the Israeli raid at Entebbe in July 1976). Airborne divisions still have jump training to keep options open and retain the cherished airborne designation. Special Forces units of all nations are jump qualified.

Many other nations joined the airborne club after the war and there have been a number of combat parachute jumps since 1945, but none on the scale of the Second World War. One reason for that was none of the wars were on the scale of the Second World War.

The epitome of airborne is still parachute infantry. Today, more than forty nations award Jump Wings, but their airborne units are small. In the 1950s French Foreign Legion 'Paras' went into Indochina in several large jumps. They also dropped into Algeria and at Suez. The

British too jumped to protect the Suez Canal in 1956. Dutch parachute troops dropped in Indonesia in 1948. Israelis' jumped during the 1956 war with Egypt to secure a key pass. There were several small unit combat jumps in Vietnam by US Special Forces and Army Combat Teams. Larger efforts were the US Ranger jump at Granada in 1983 and 1989 Ranger/82nd AD drops in Panama. In 2003 a battalion of 508th PIR was dropped into Northern Iraq. None of those operations approached the multiple division-size operations of US and British airborne units in 1943-1945.

Earning Jump Wings is still highly prized by all services,[25] but operational employment of airborne infantry is back to specialized small unit ops where it was in the beginning. New jump techniques let a single plane at high altitude drop small teams of men who free-fall to low altitude before opening their chutes. With specially designed chutes a fully armed jumper can land, standing up, on a target smaller than a four-foot circle, but today troops would just as likely go in as Air Assault troops on low-flying stealth helicopters like the SEAL team that killed Osama bin Laden in 2013.

A lot has changed in warfare in seven decades, but airborne determination, pride, glory, and traditions[26] forged during the Second World War burn just as bright today in infantry who go to battle vertically.

US Navy

US Army

French Second World War Wings

German Second World War Wings

---

25. When I attended my daughter's Jump Graduation Ceremony at Fort Benning, GA in 1985 her class had men and women, and Marines as well as US Army. The only thing more highly prized than jump wings was having 'mustard' on your wings—a star for a combat jump (an award approved in 1983).

26. For example, each September 82nd Airborne Division Engineer Companies race 14-man Zodiac boats five laps across a lake at Fort Bragg, NC, celebrating the heroic multiple round-trip lifts under fire of riflemen over the Waal at Nijmegen on 18 September 1944.

MAPS

OVERLORD EAST

British 6th Airborne Division
6 June 1944

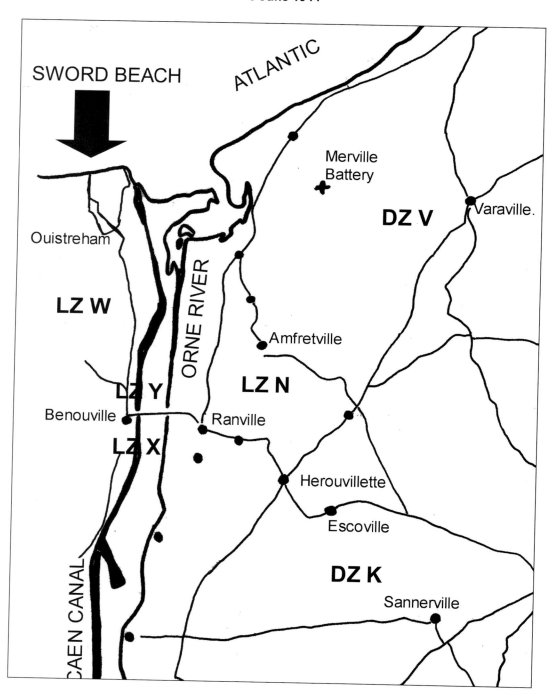

OVERLORD WEST

US 82nd Airborne Division
US 101st Airborne Division
6 June 1944

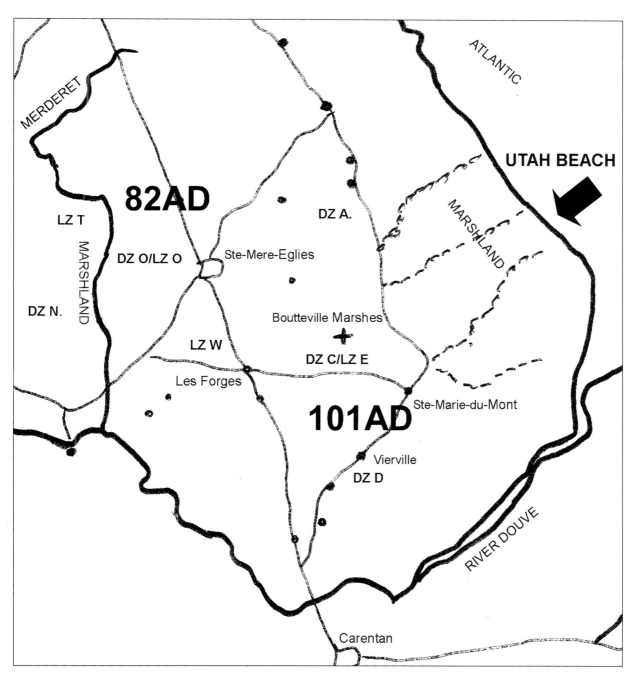

MARKET GARDEN

British 1st Airborne Division
US 82nd Airborne Division
US 101st Airborne Division
17 September 1944

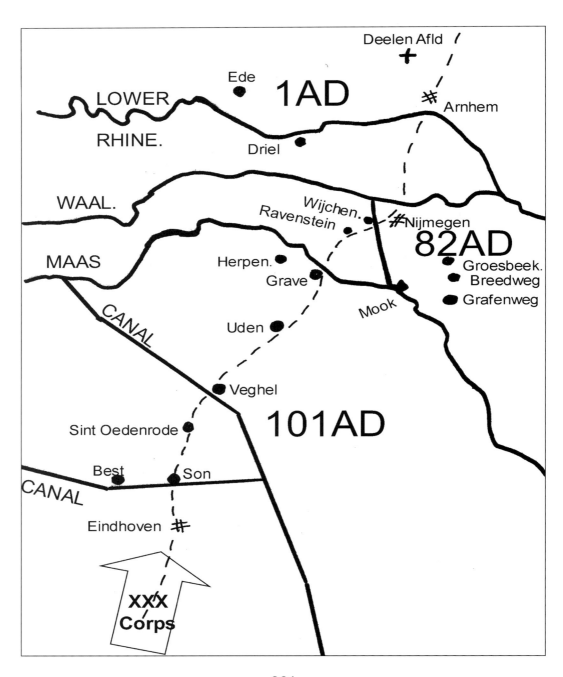

OPERATION VARSITY

British 6th Airborne Division
US 17th Airborne Division
24 March 1945

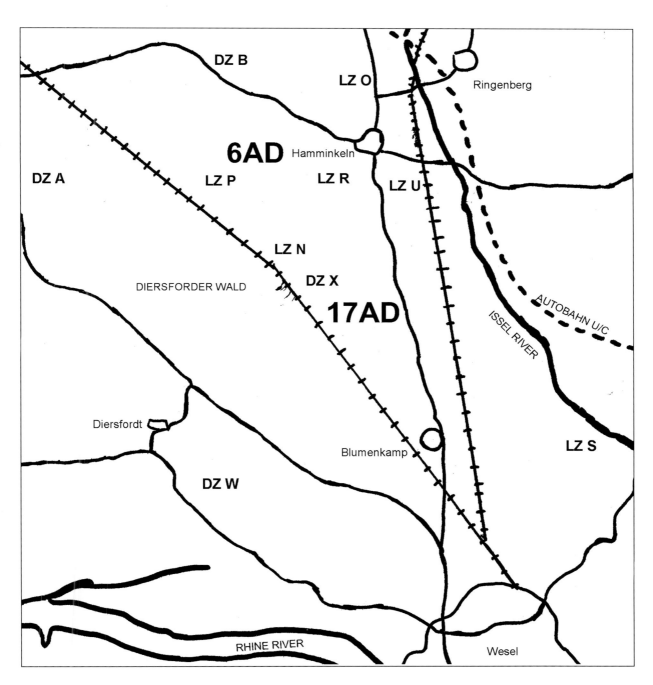

INDEX